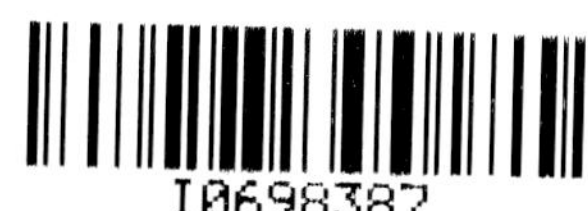

I am grateful to God for everything! And I believe that the meaning of life is to make sense of other lives.

Alessandra Dias
2024

This Book Belongs to:

Test Color Page

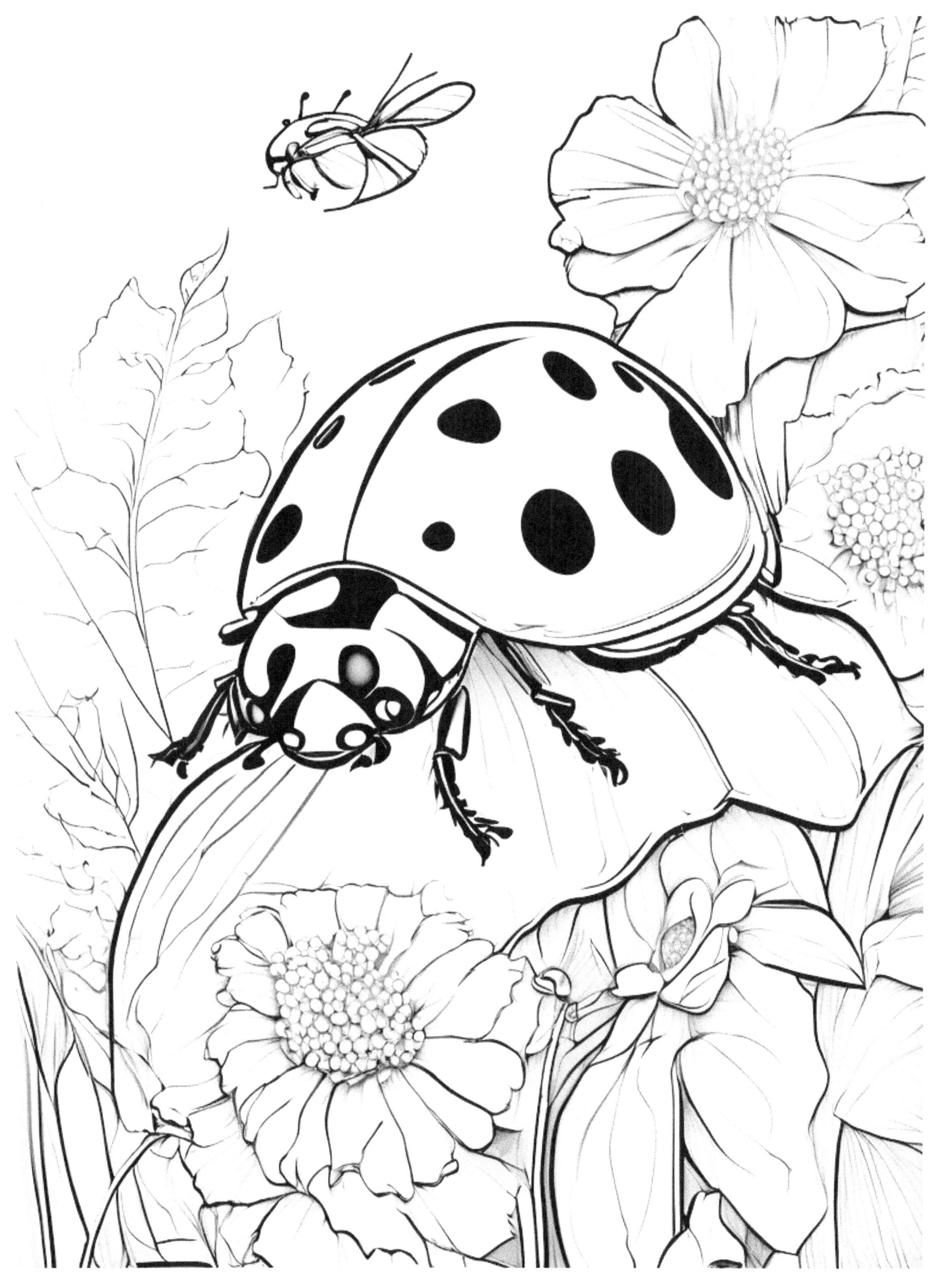

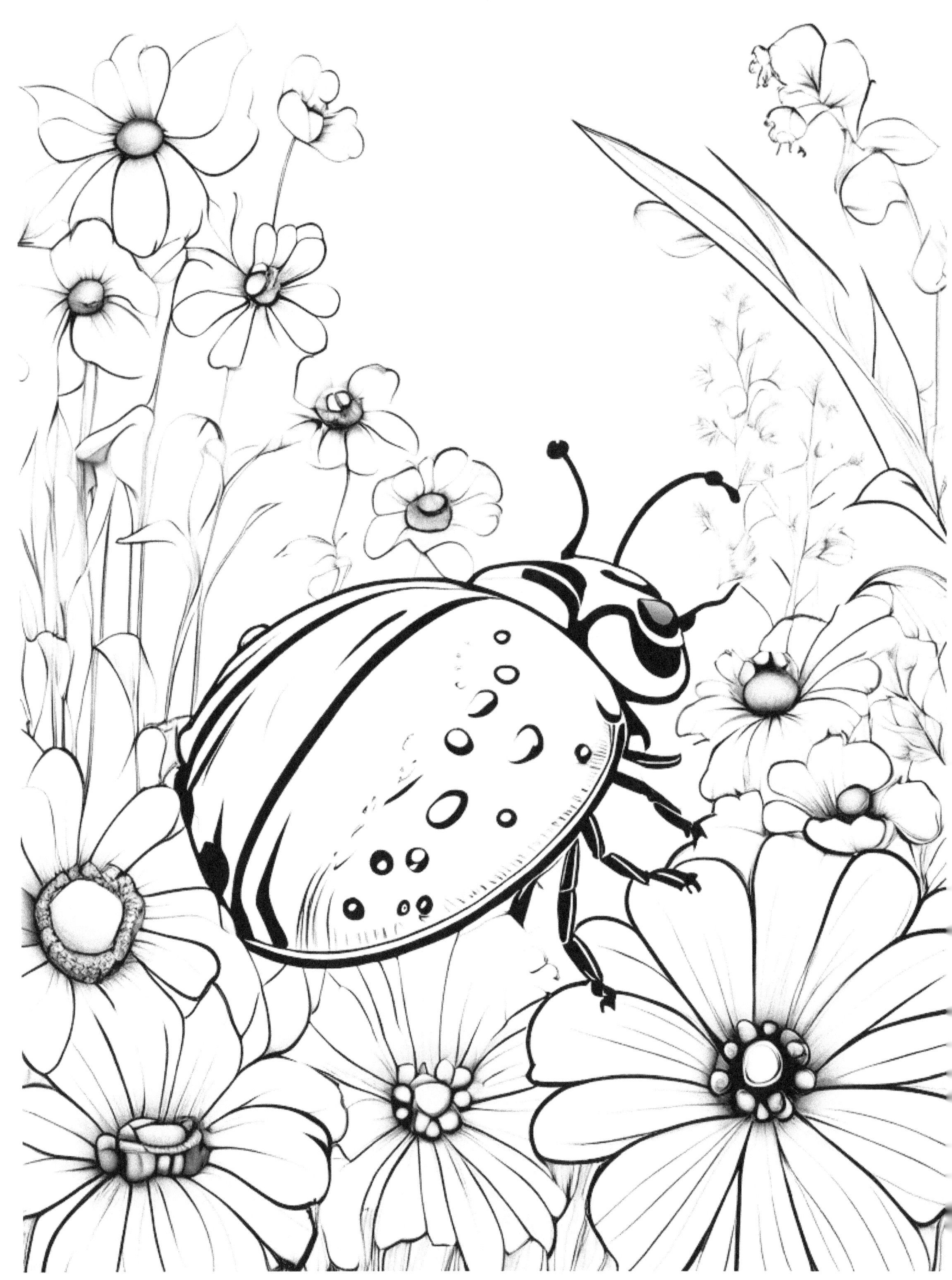

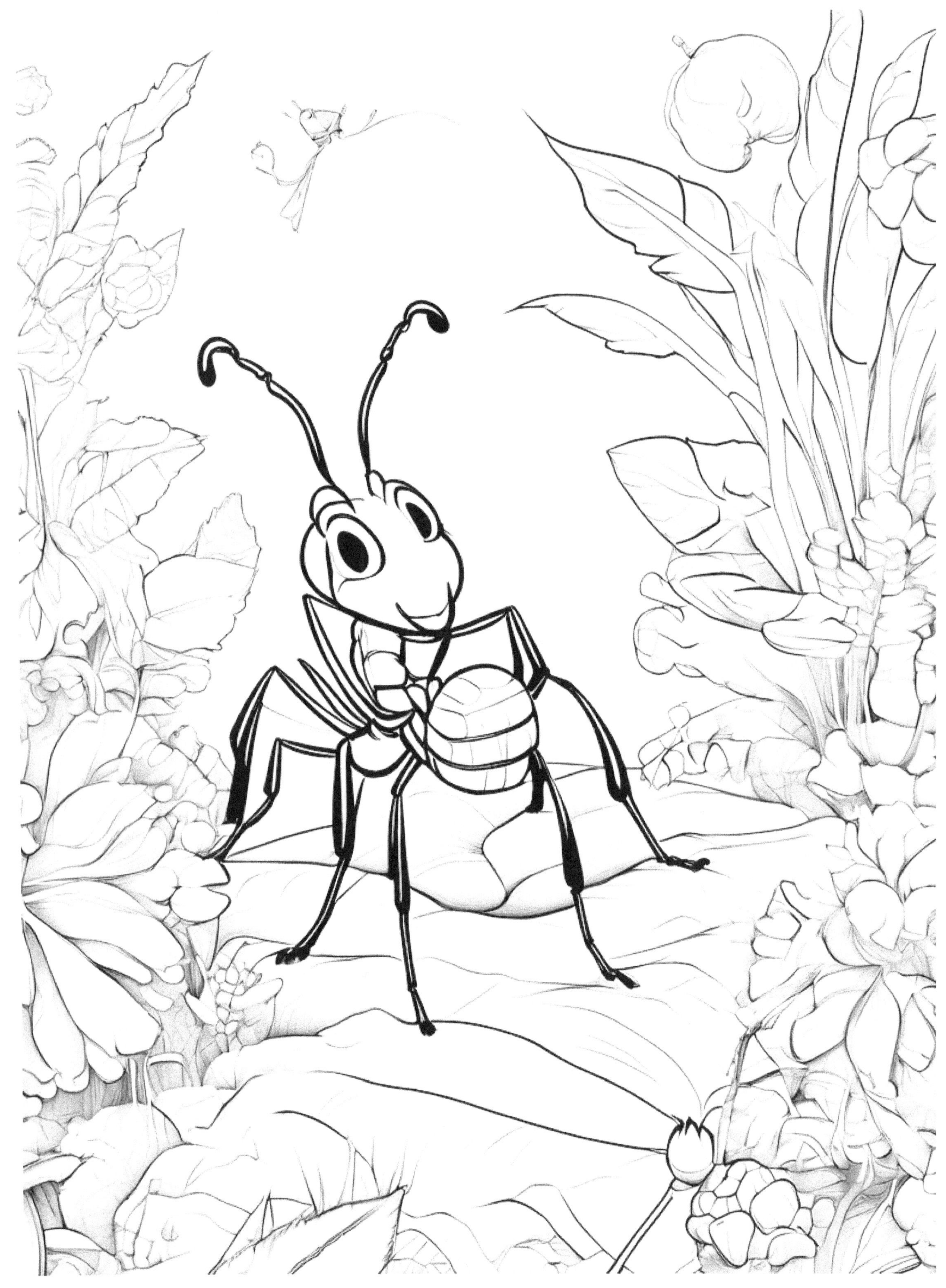

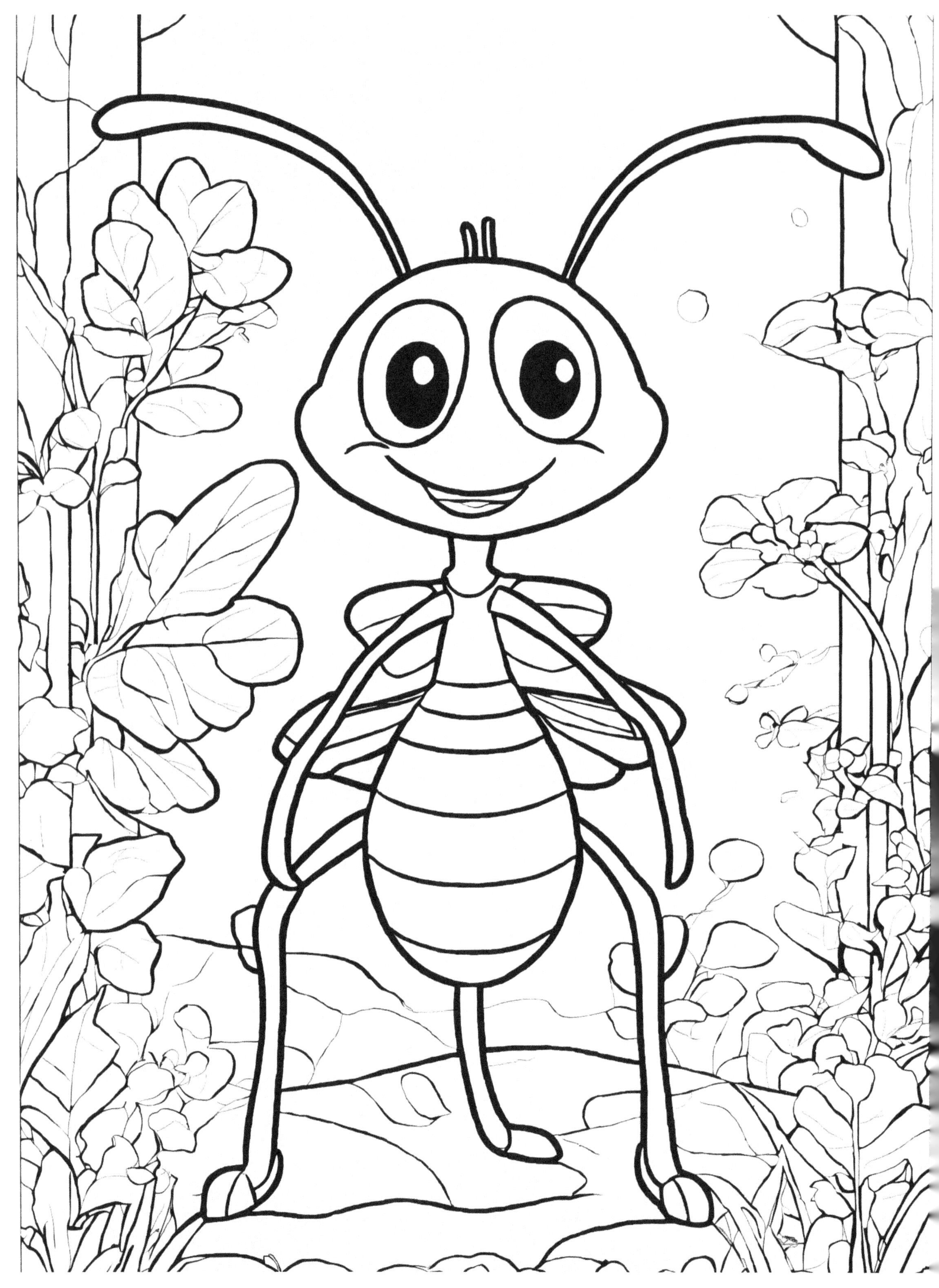

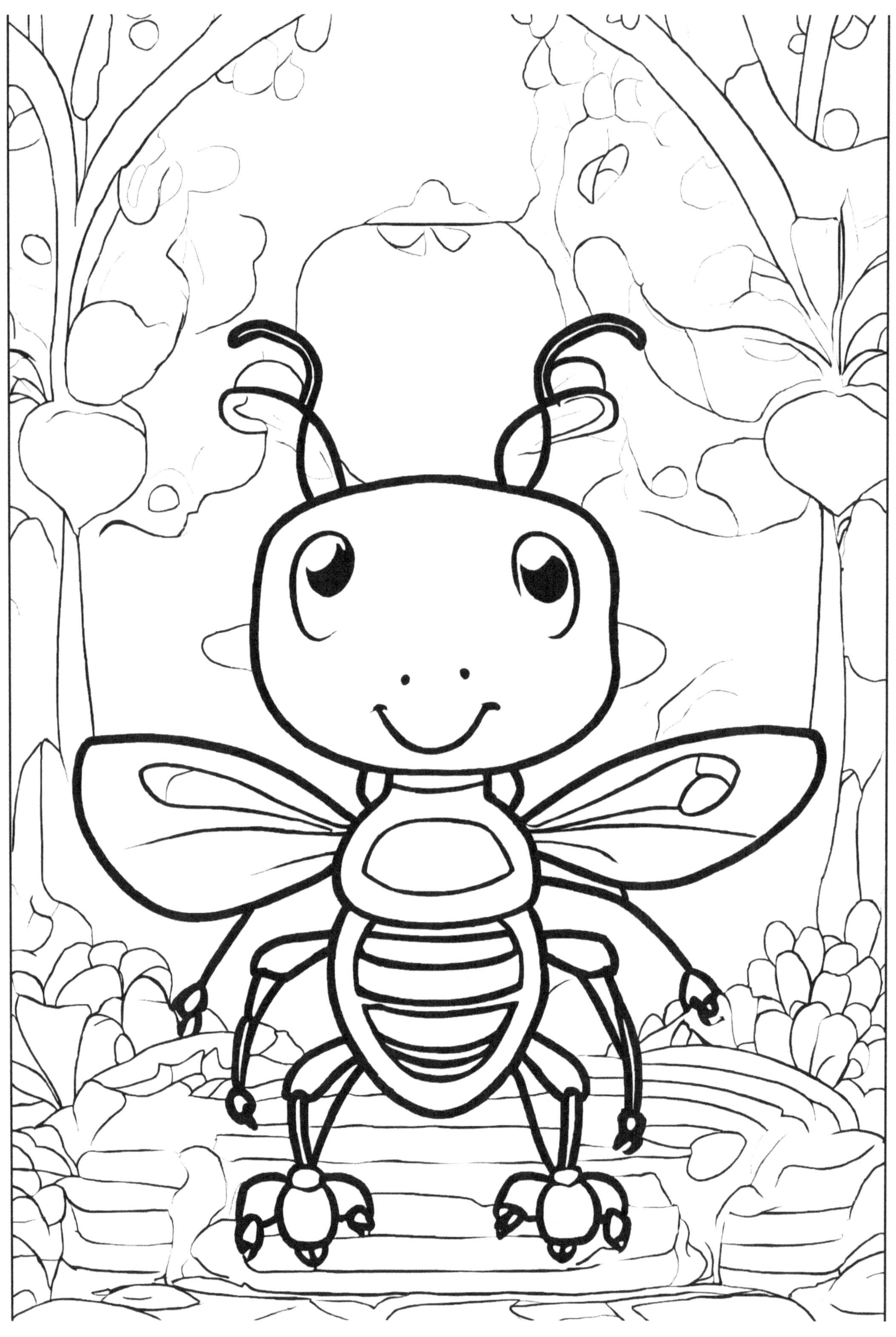

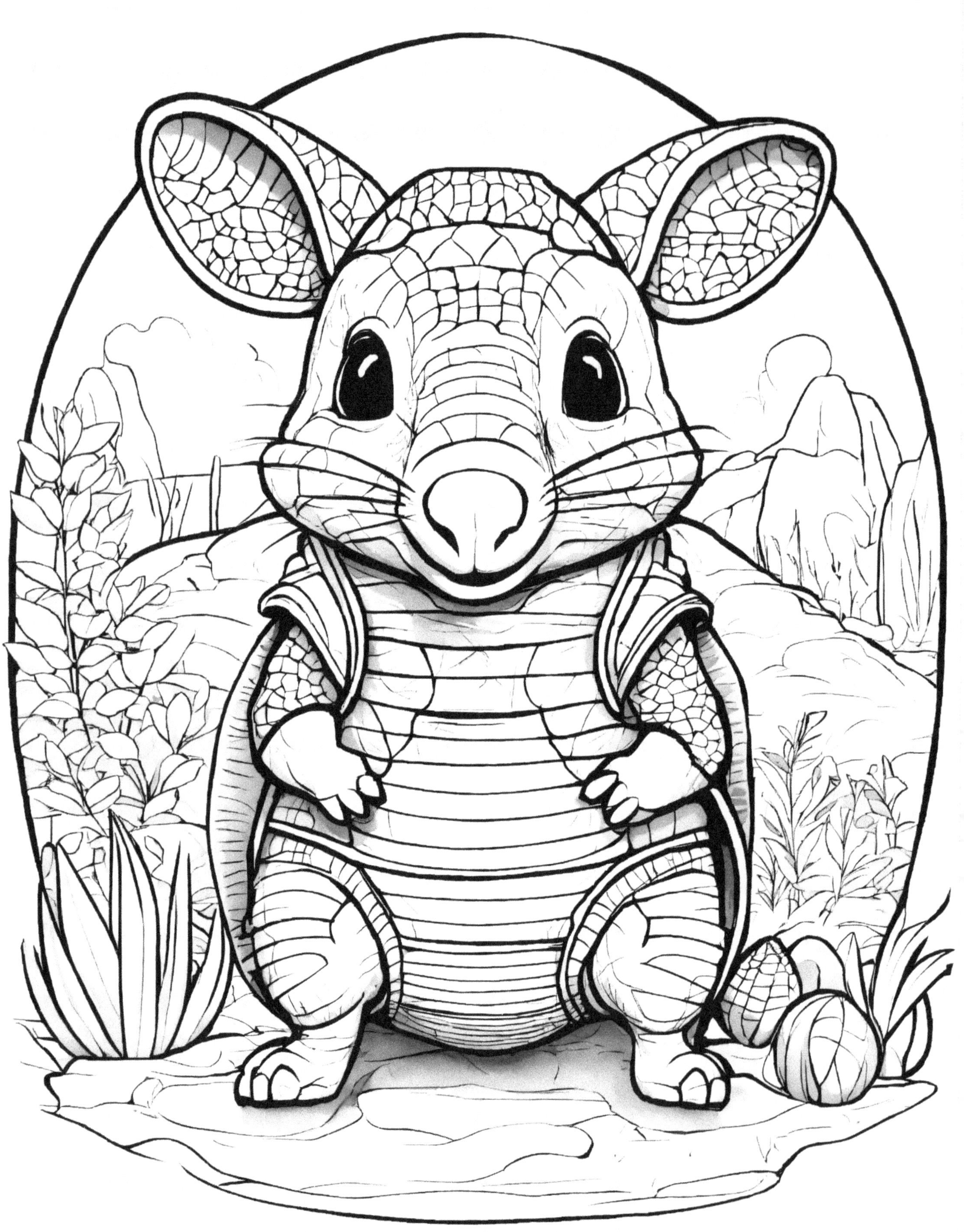

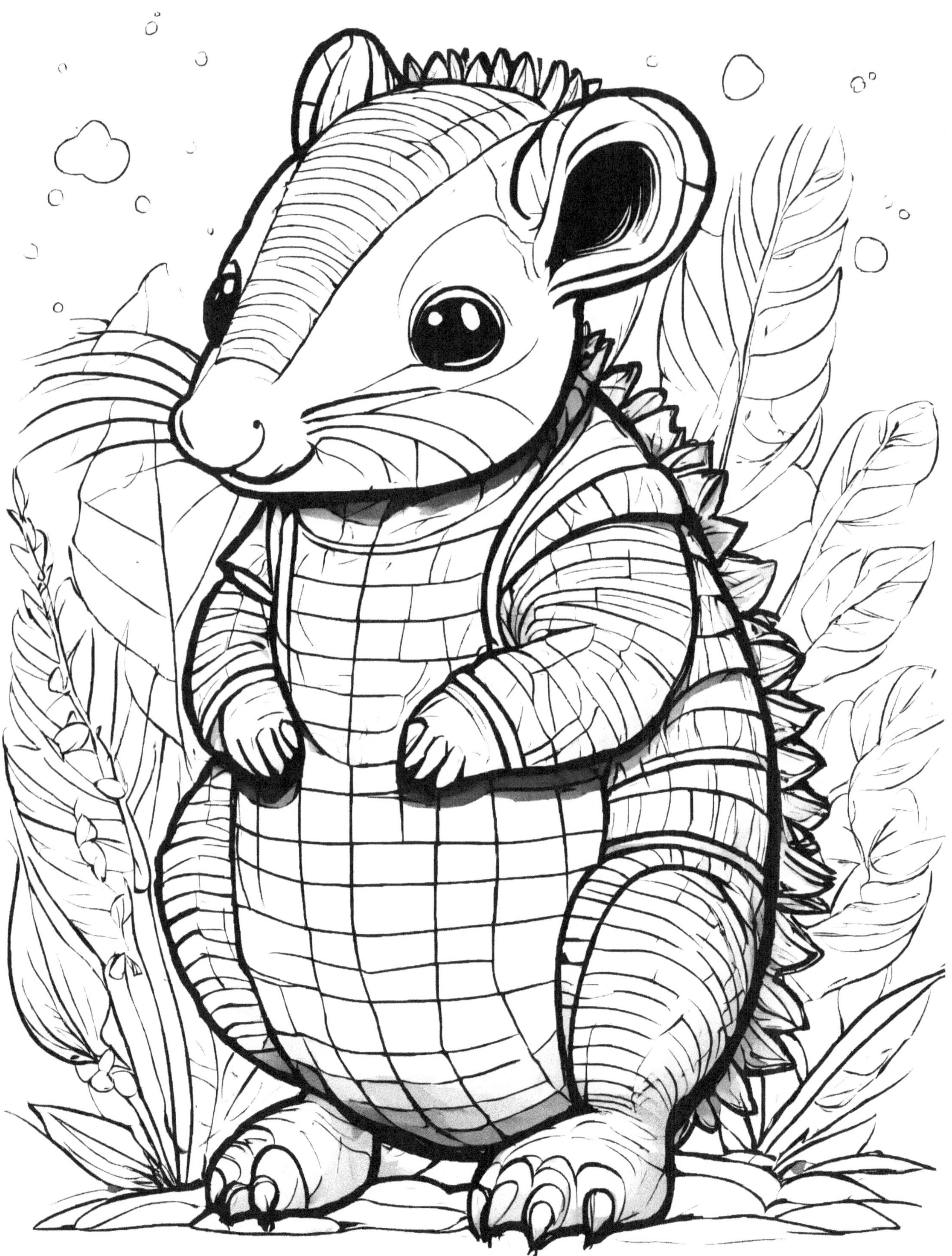

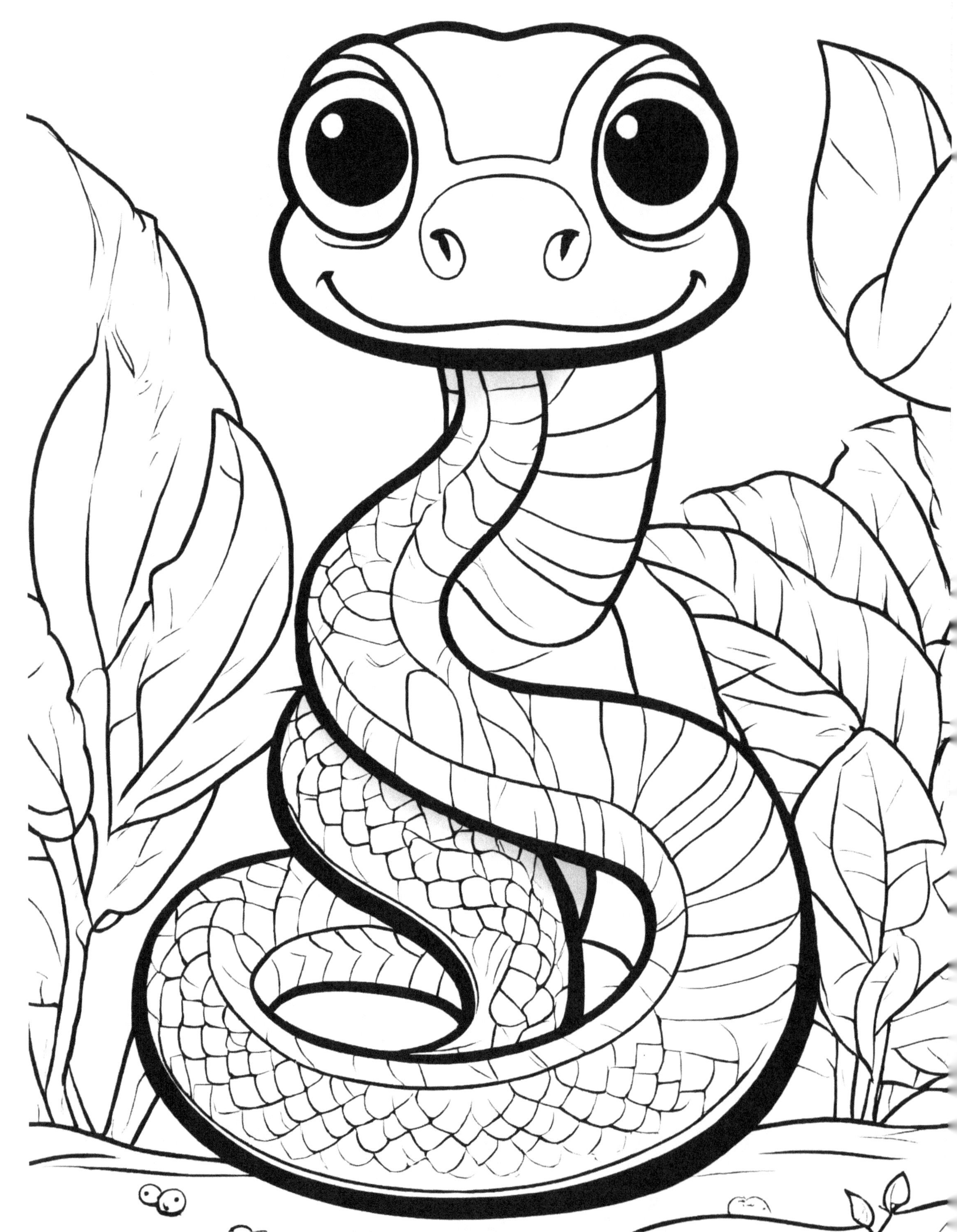

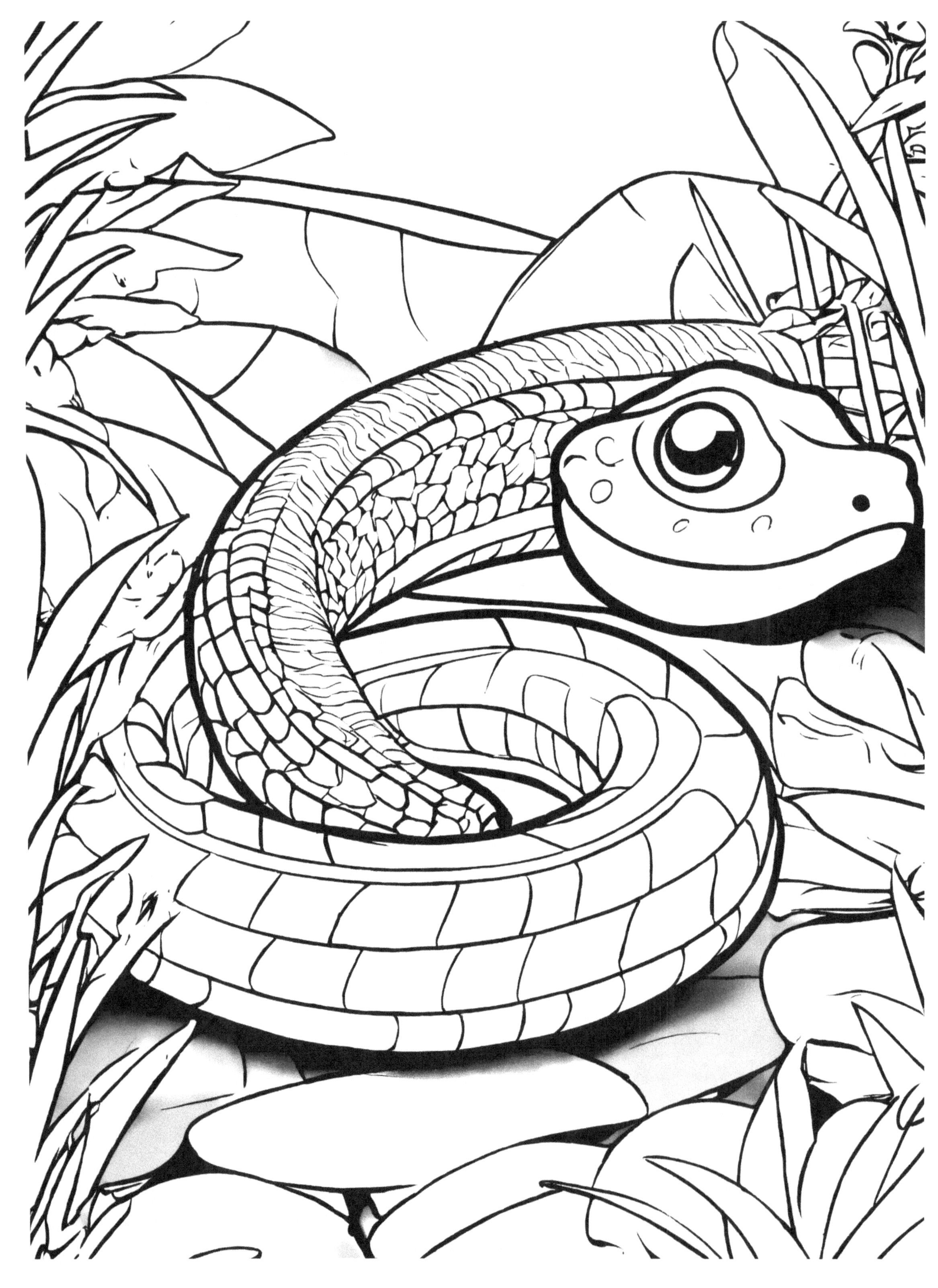

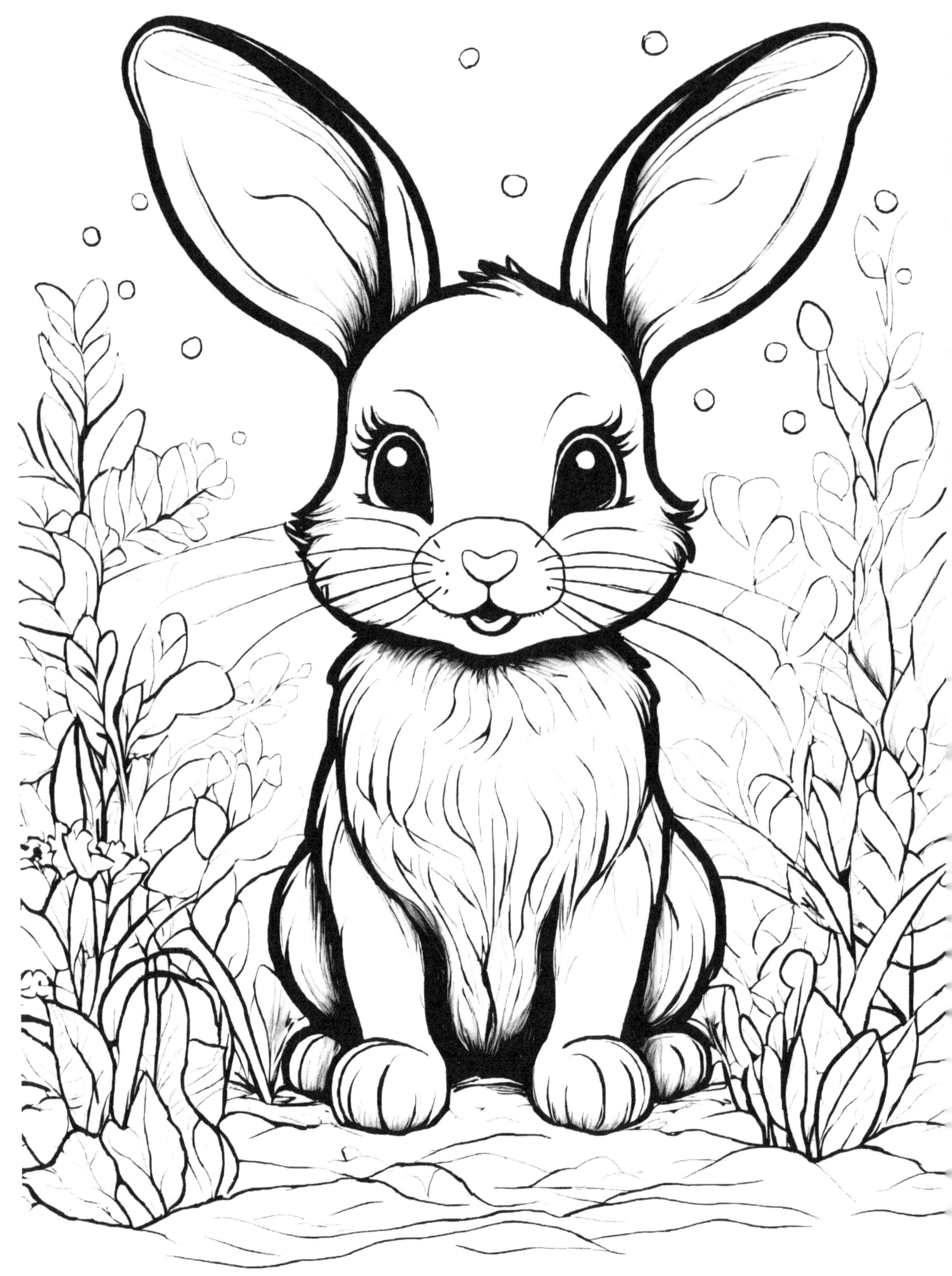

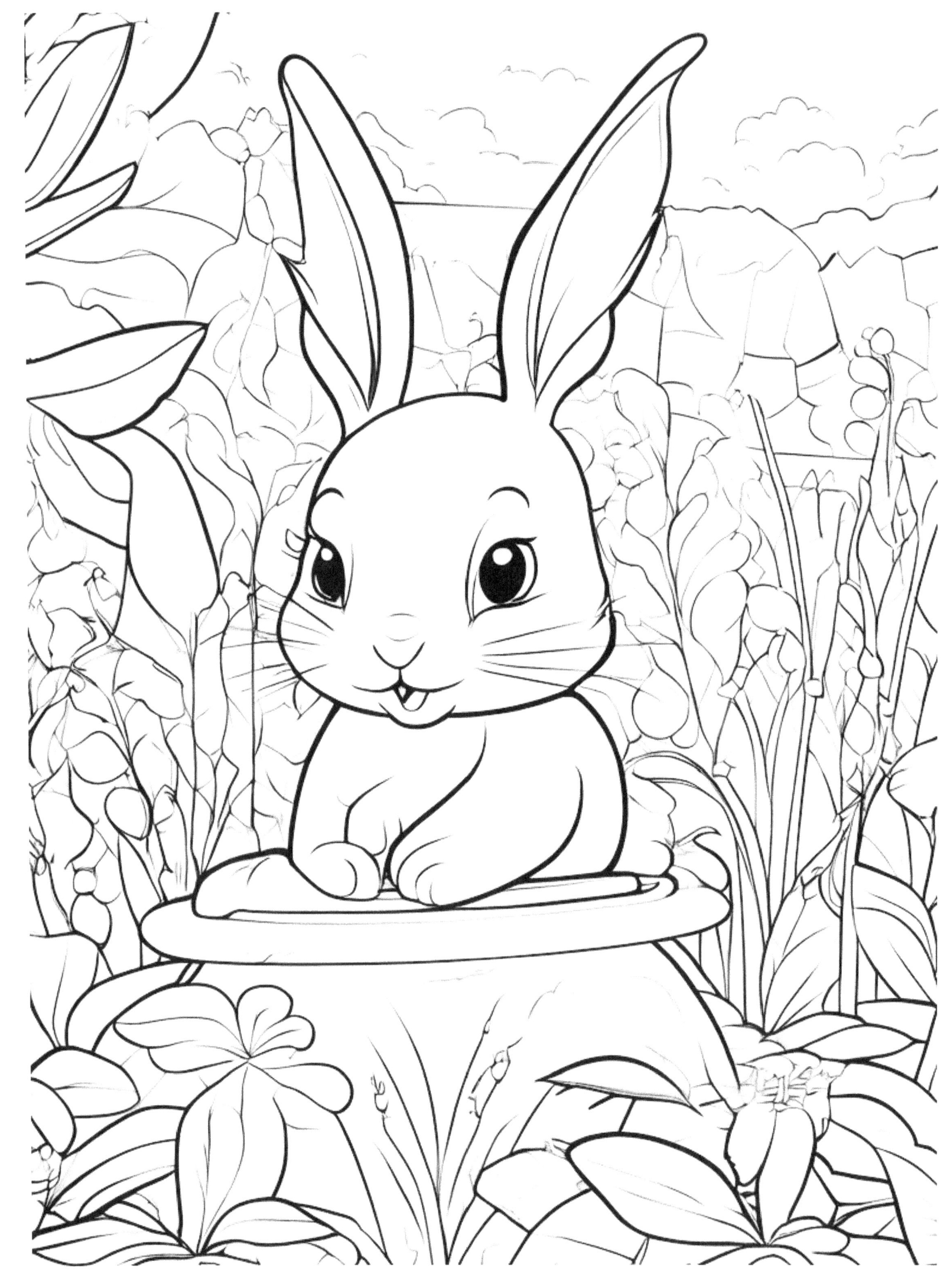

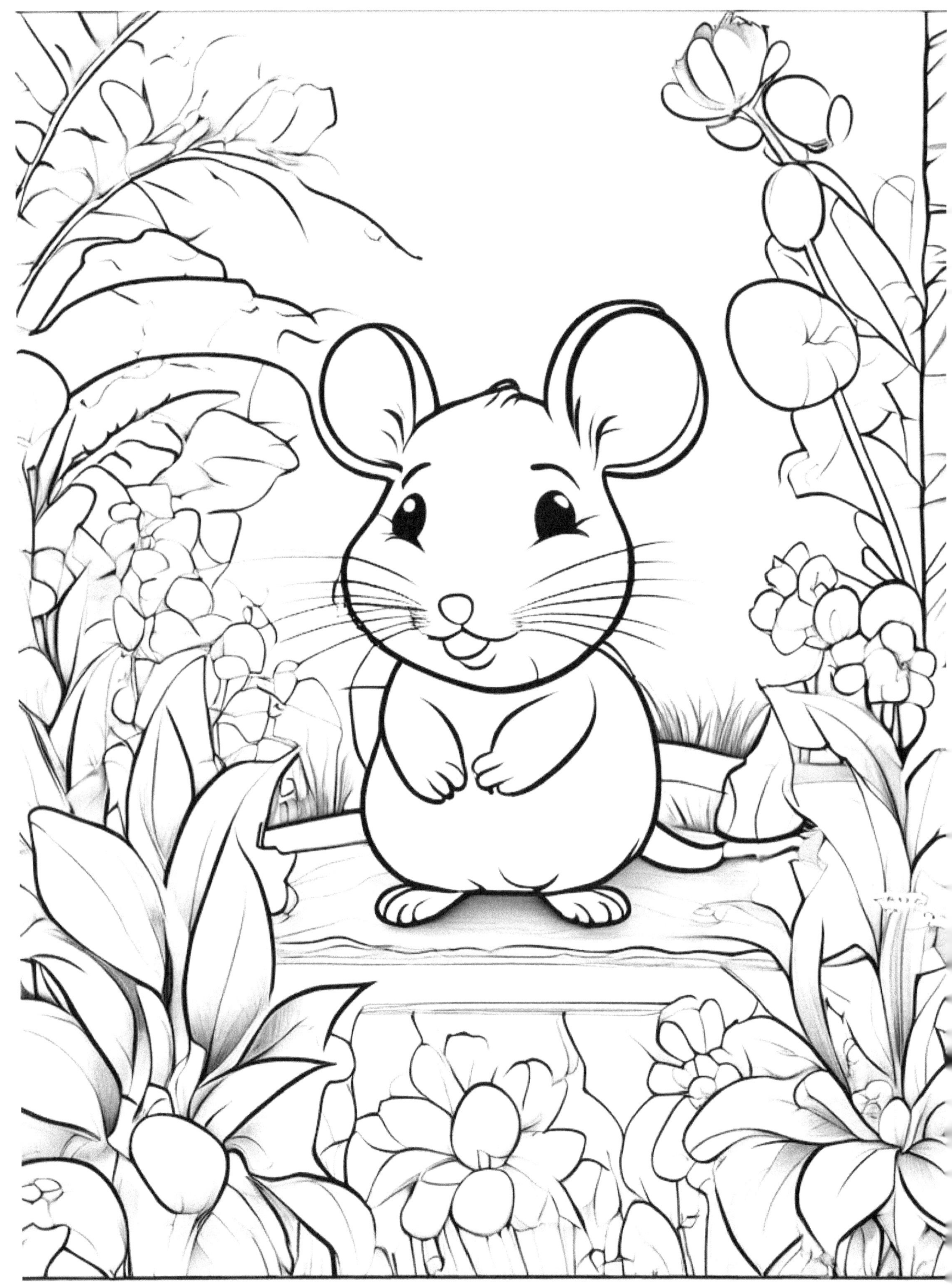

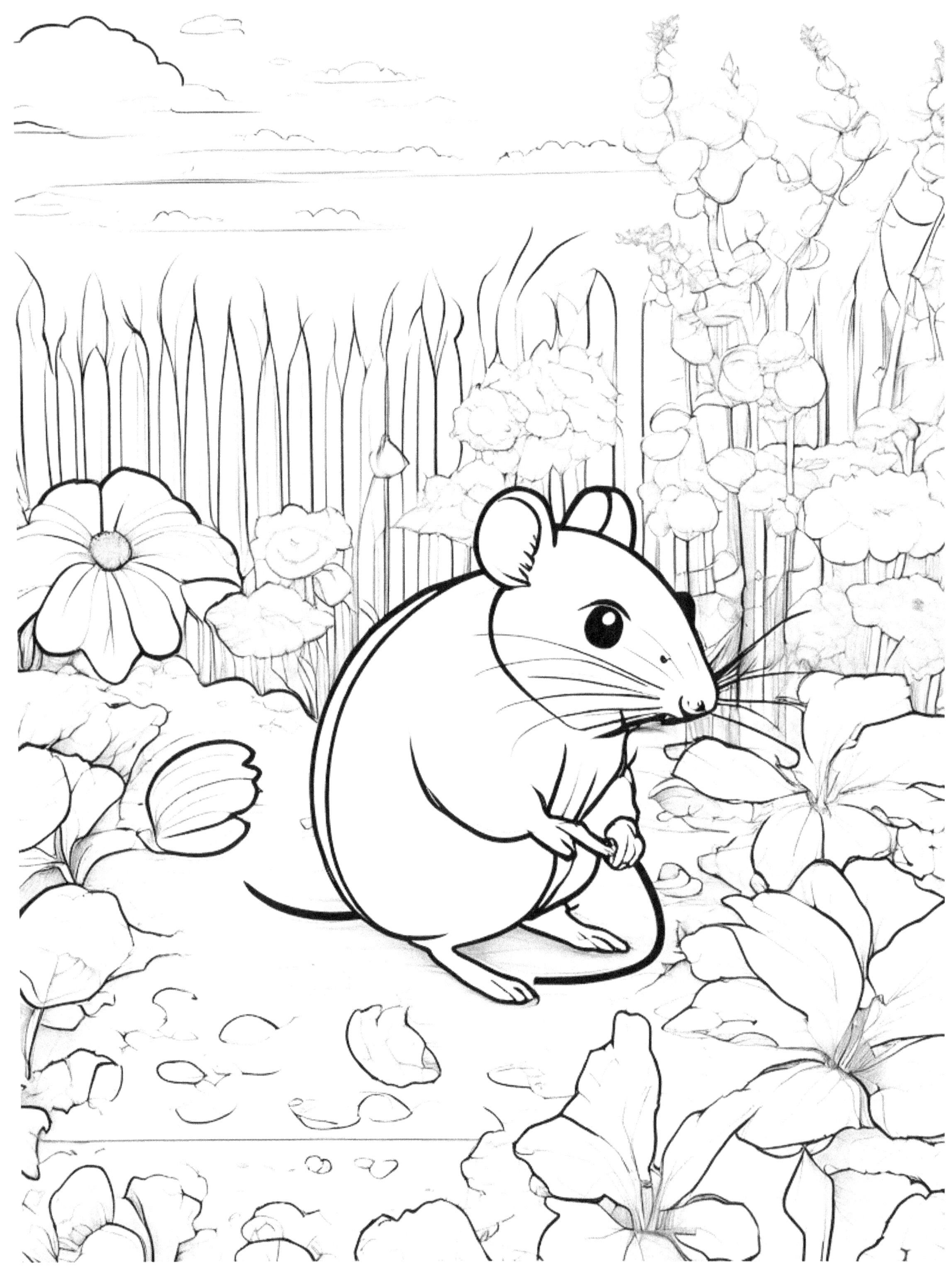

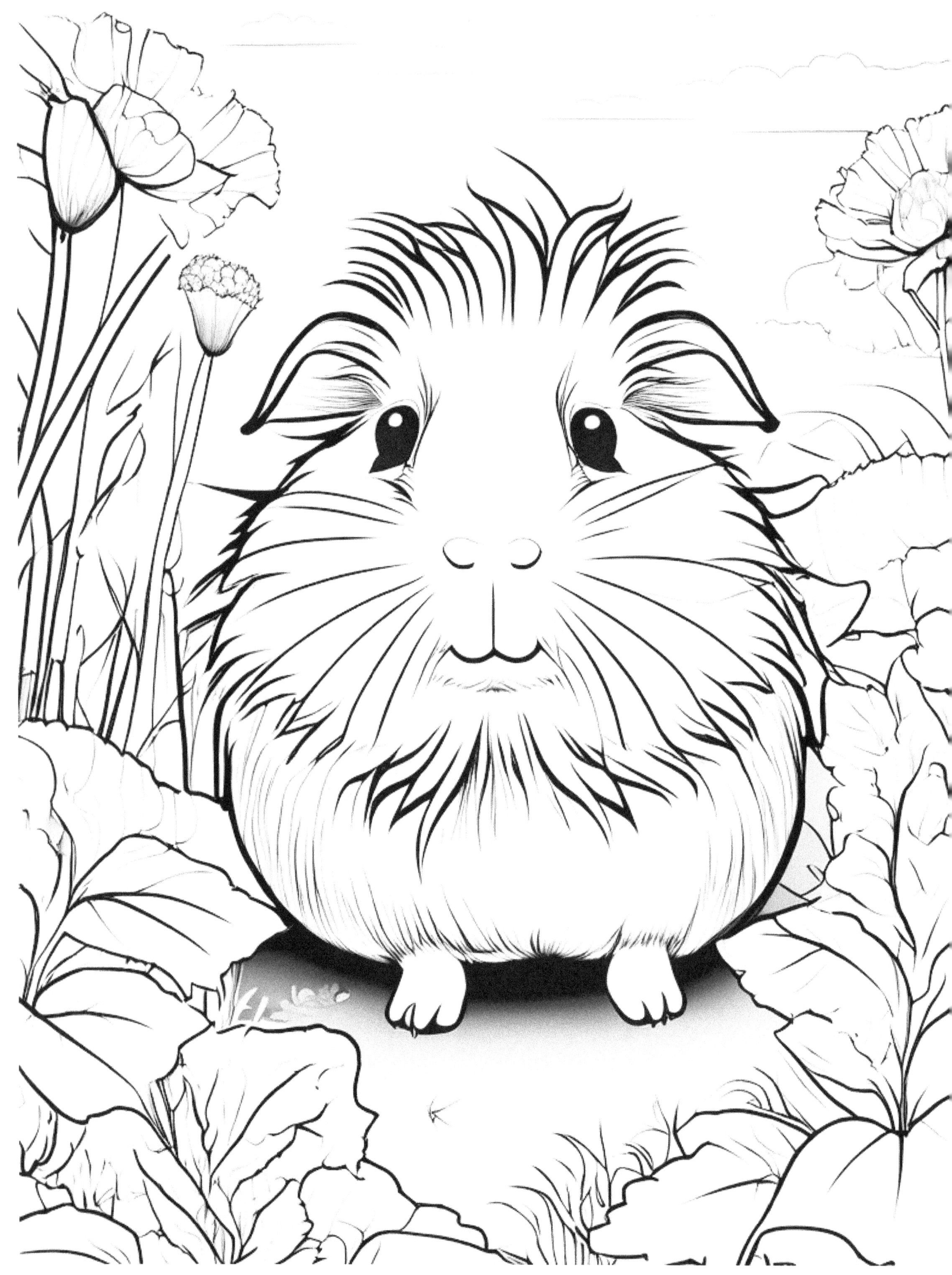

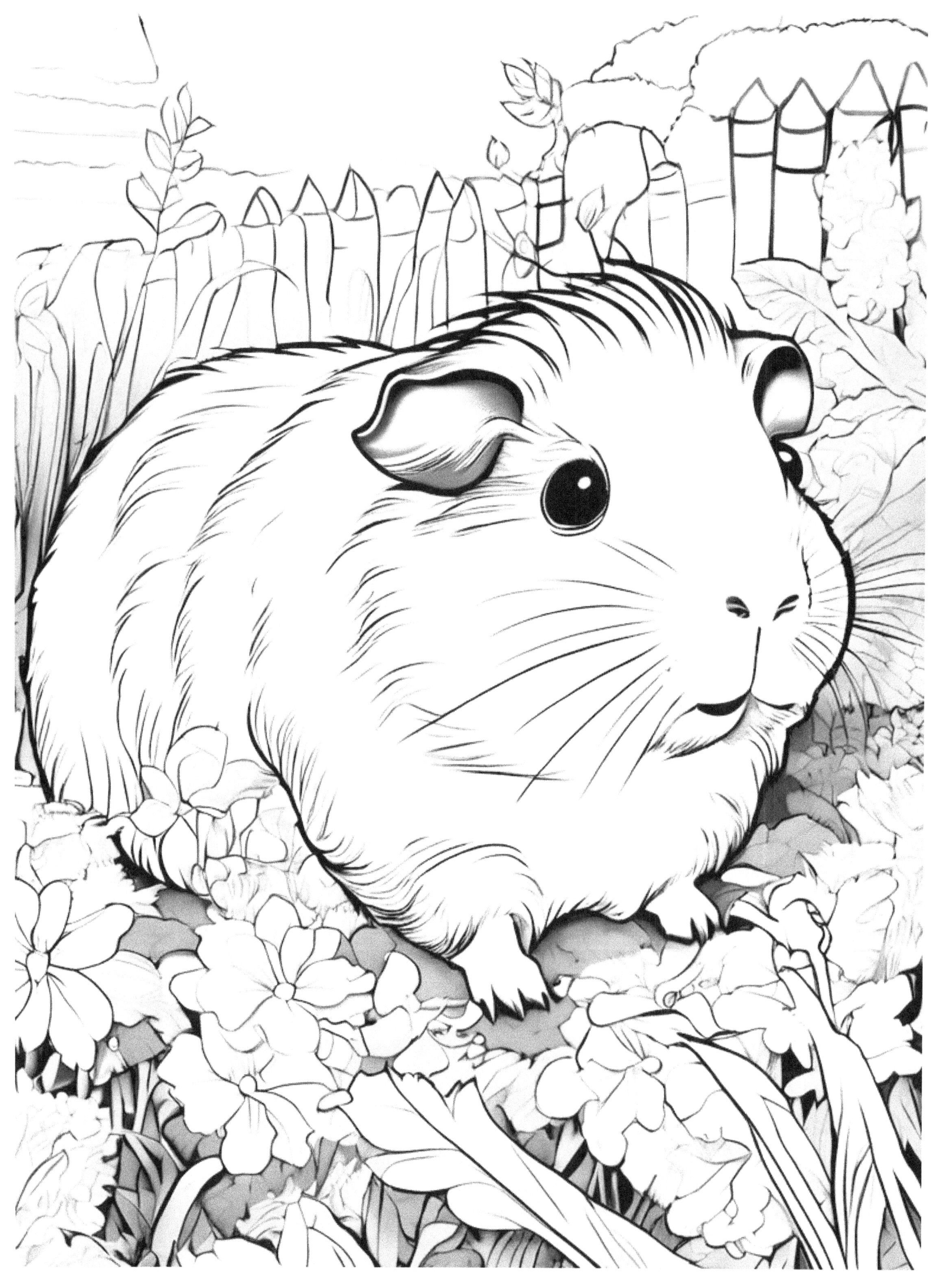

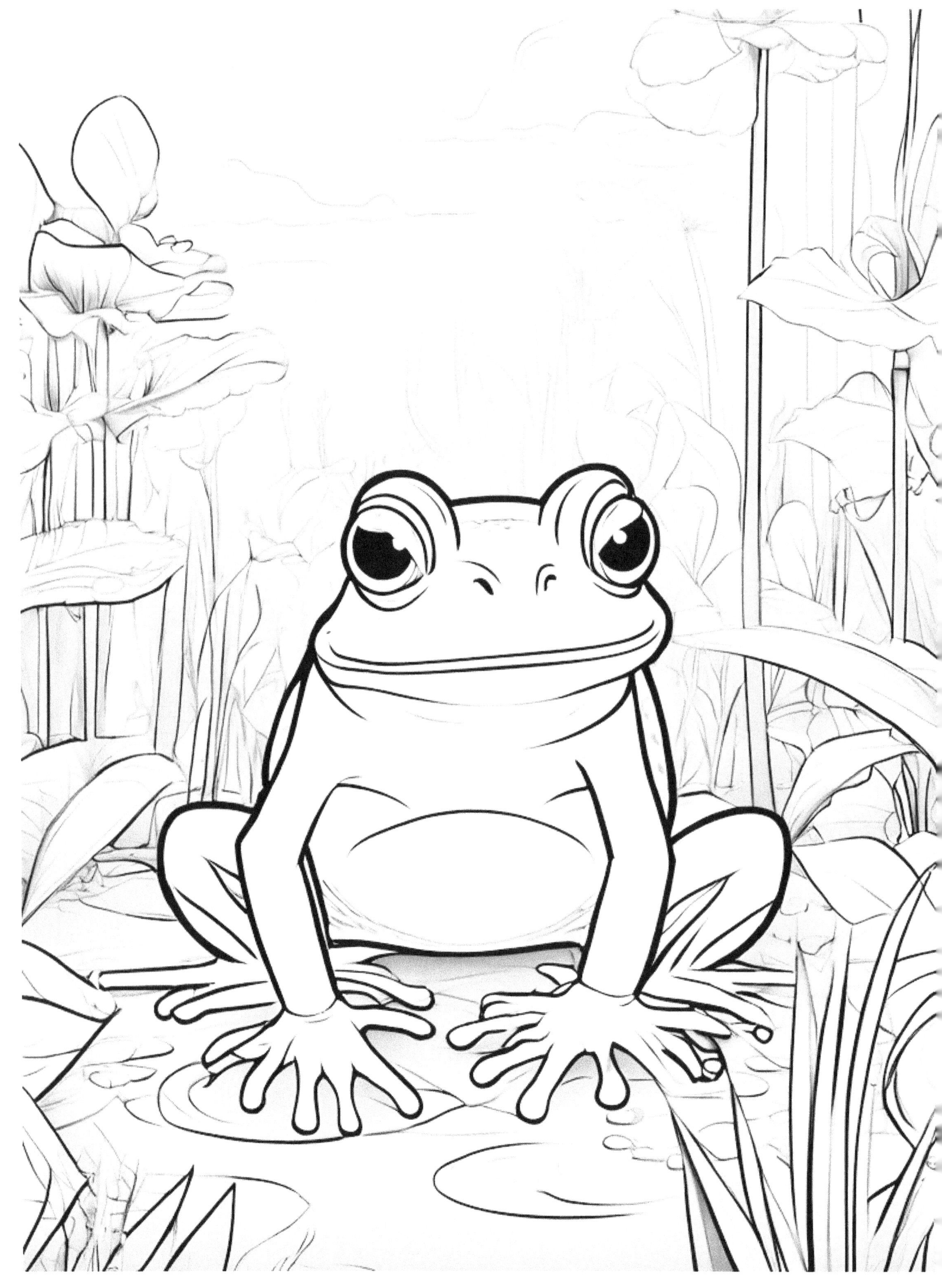

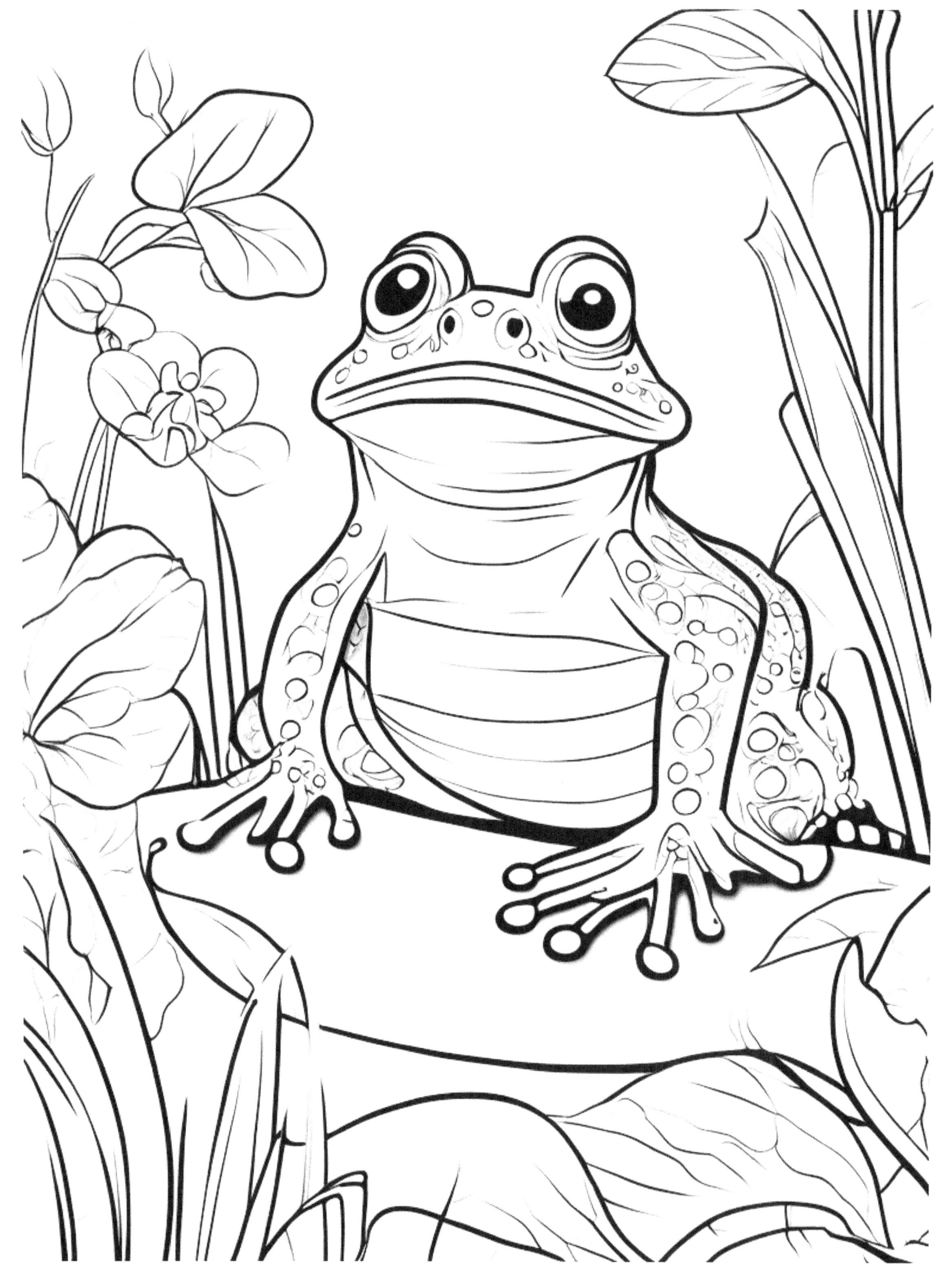

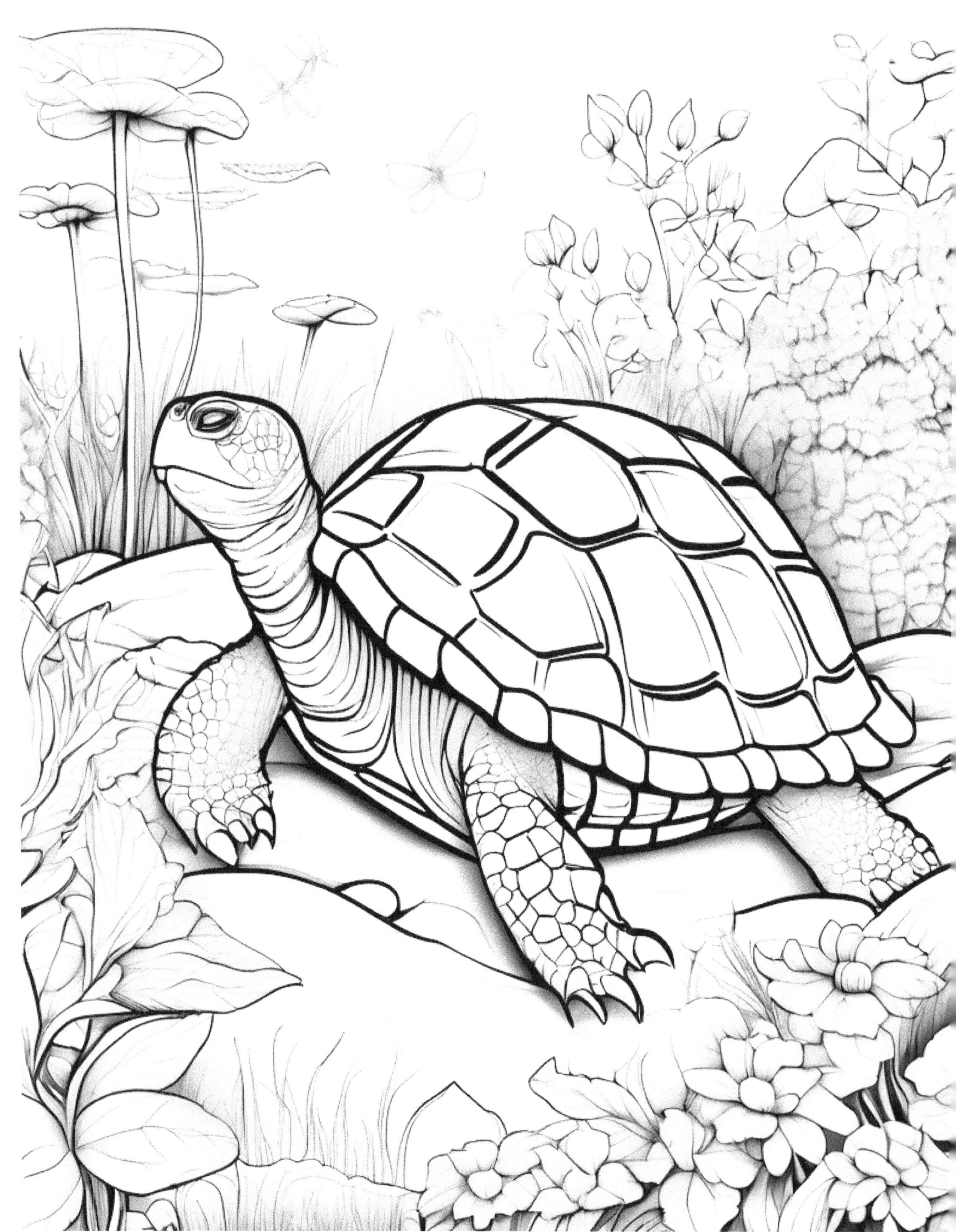

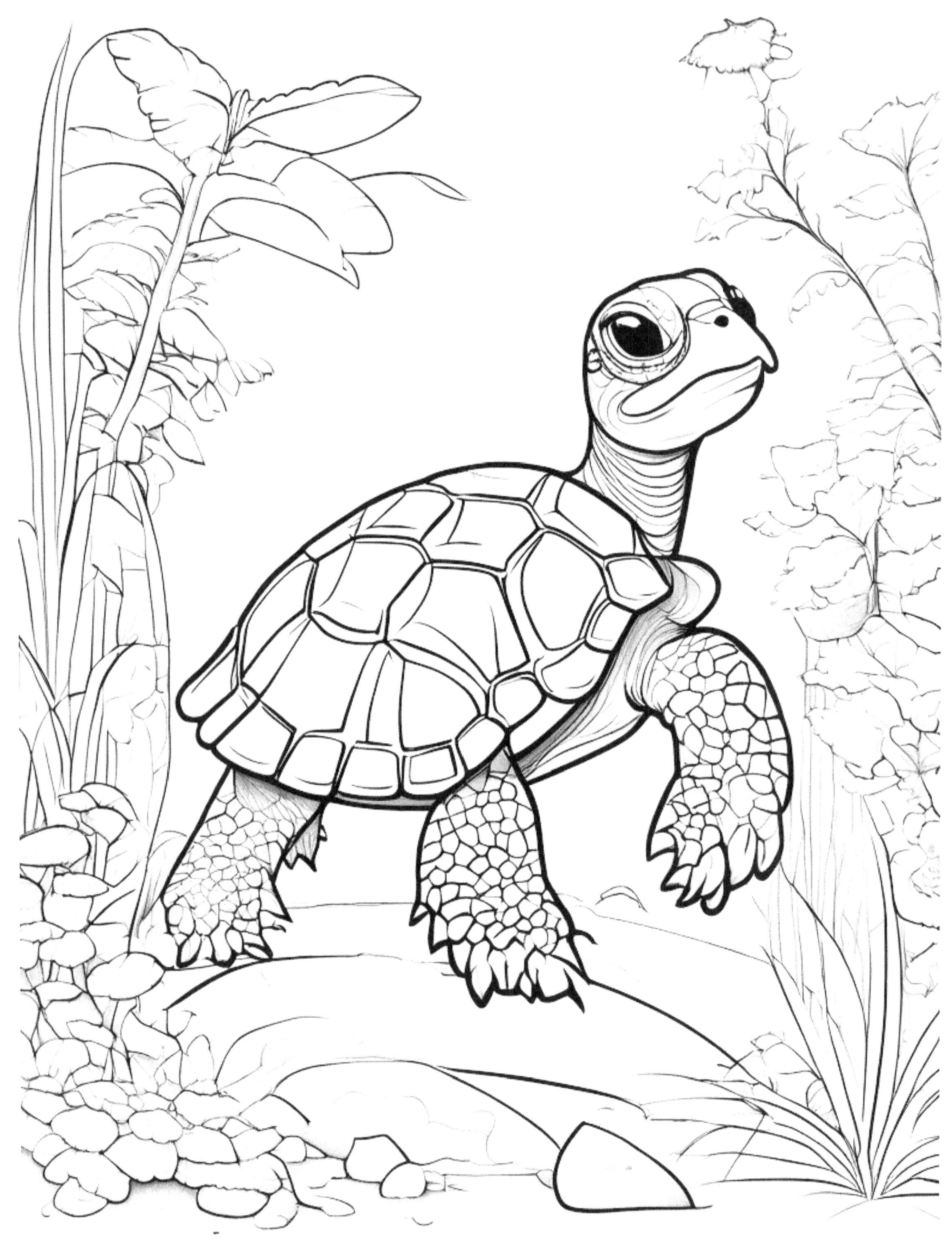

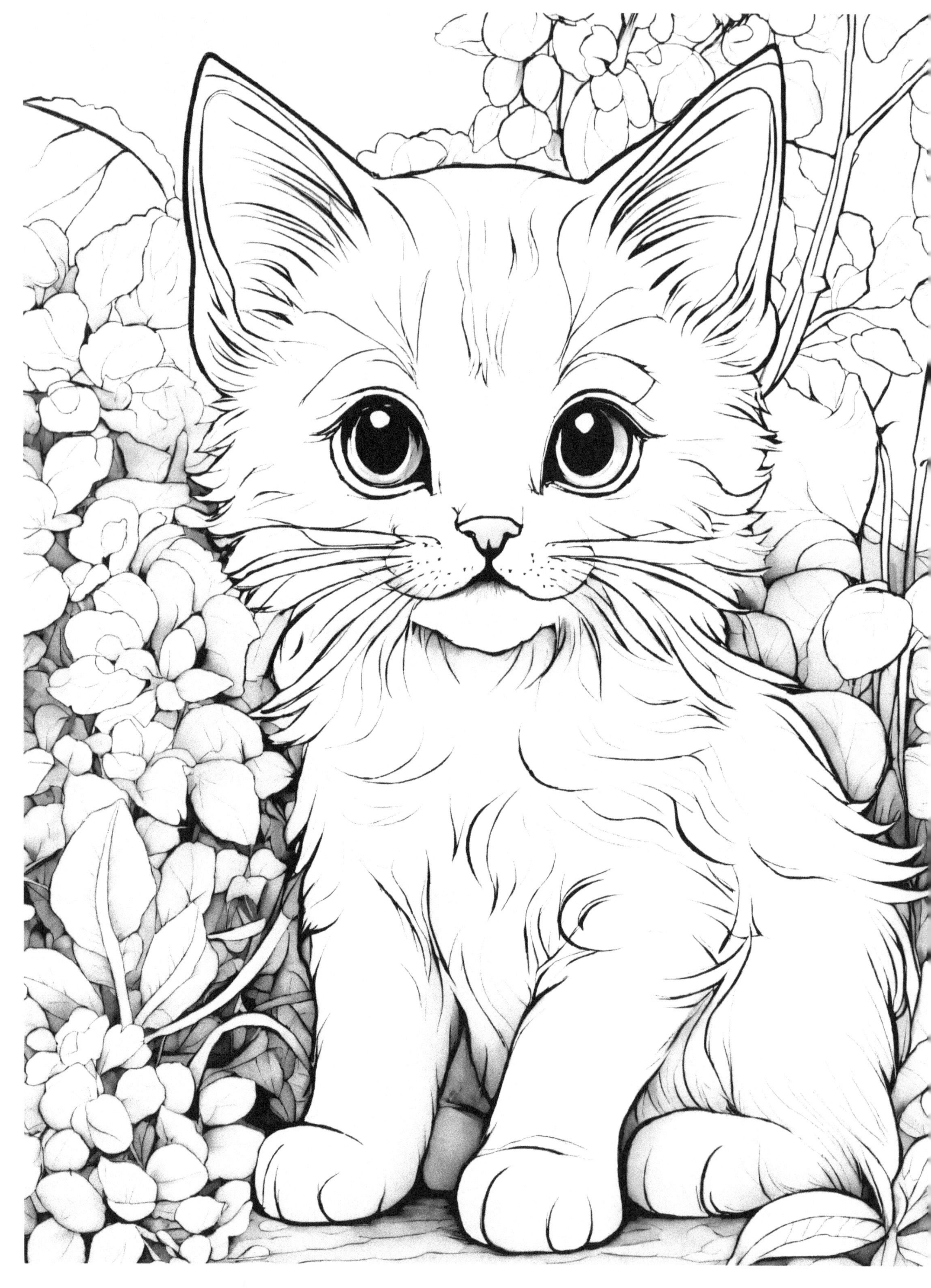

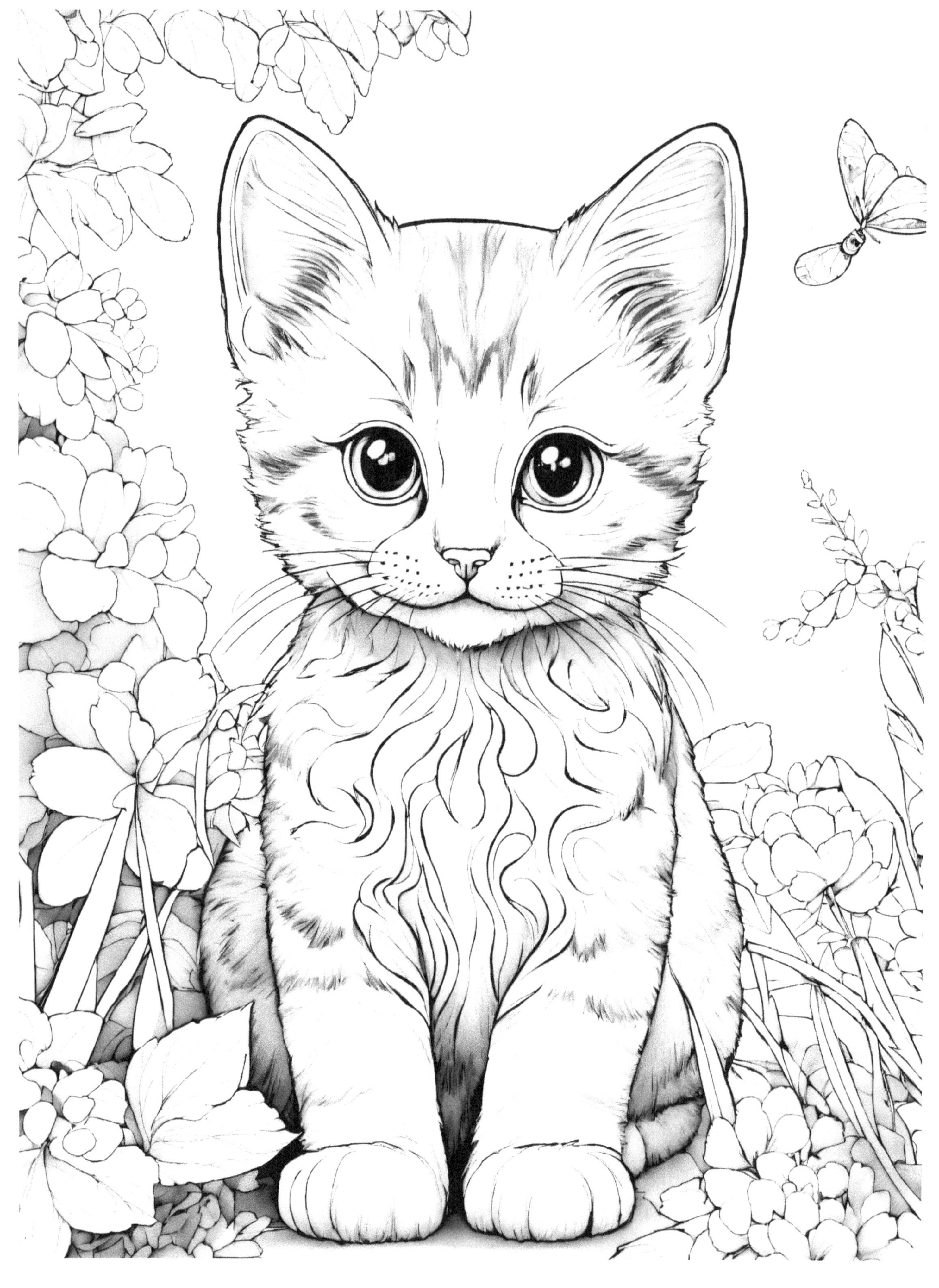

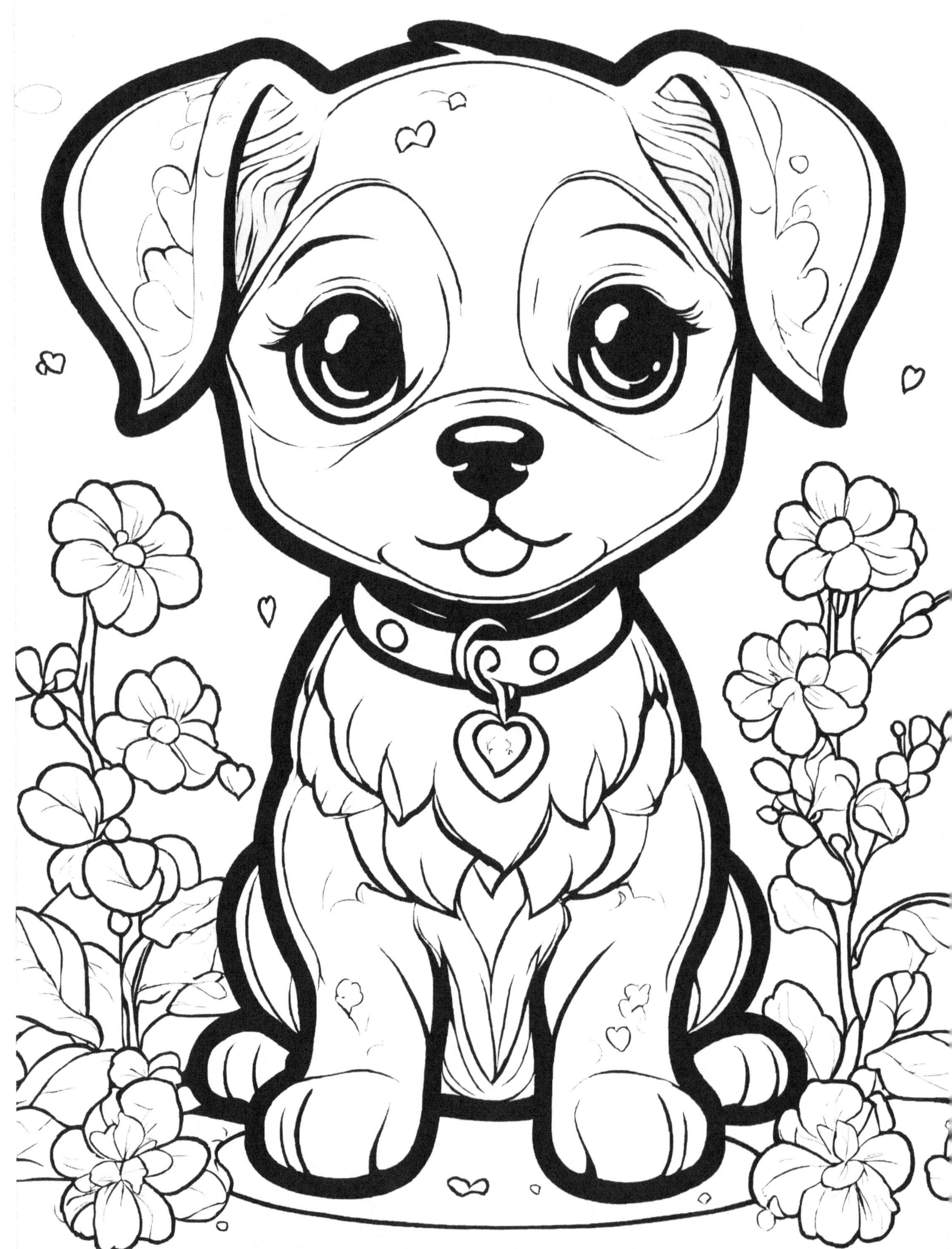

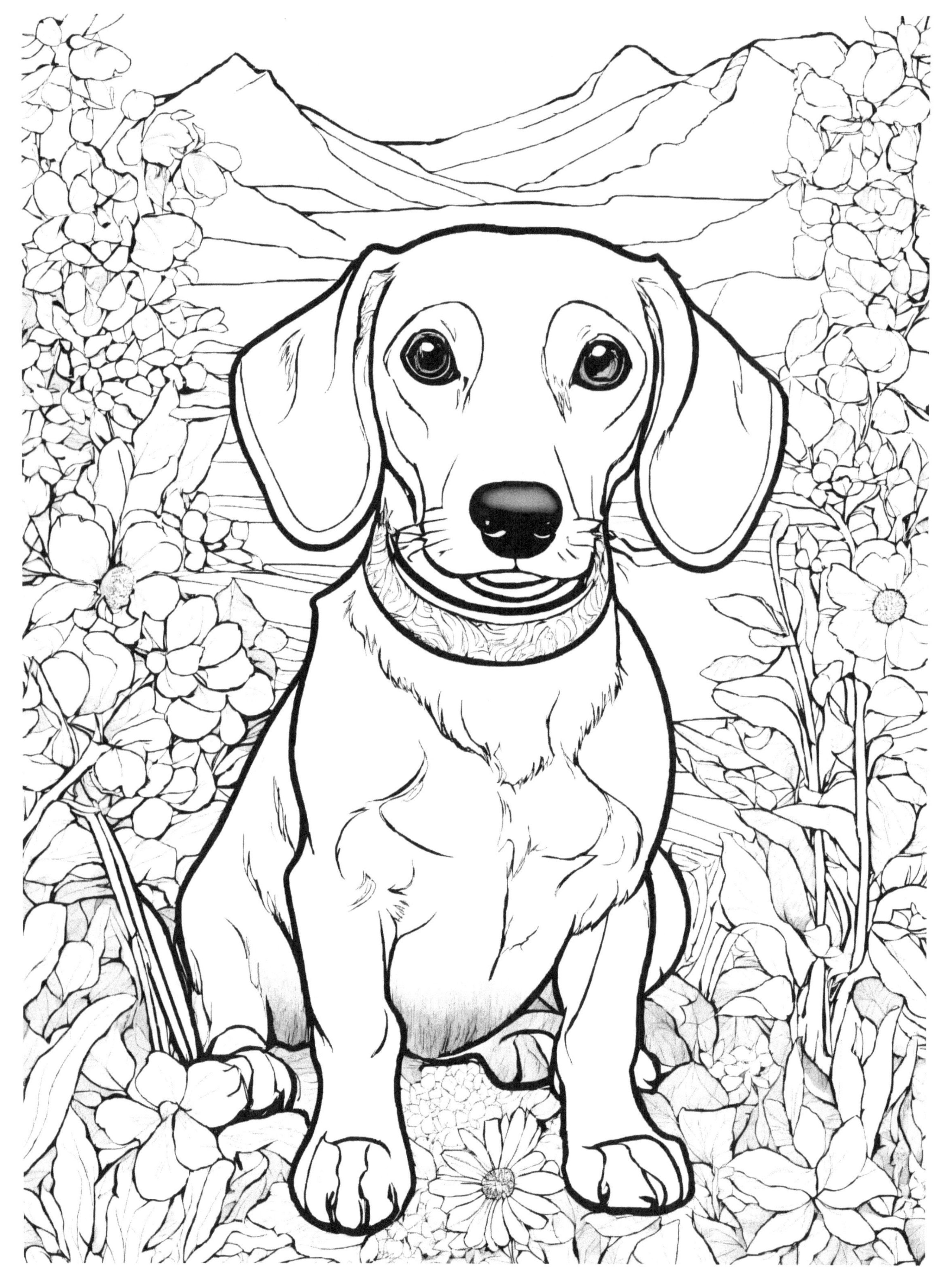

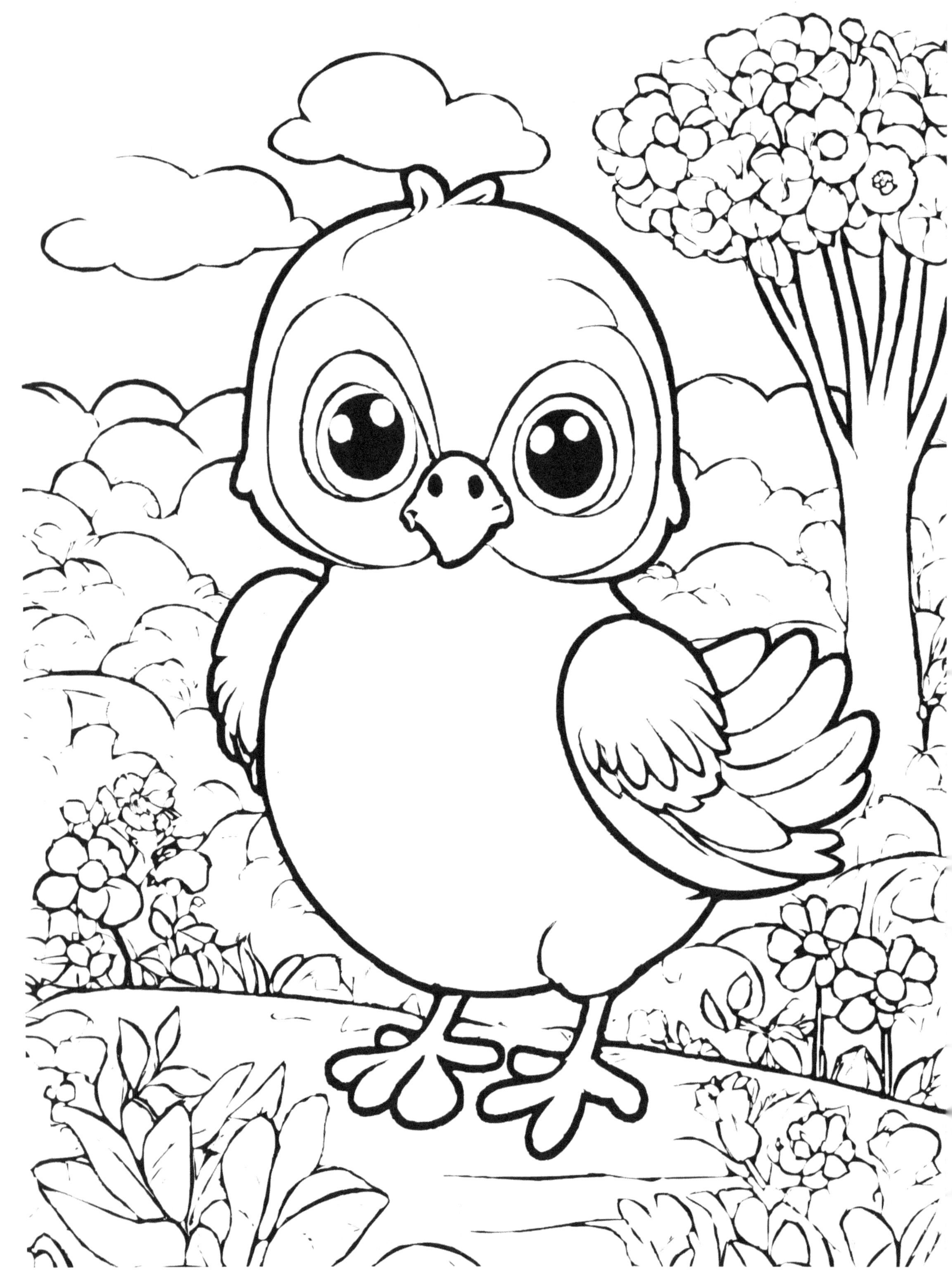

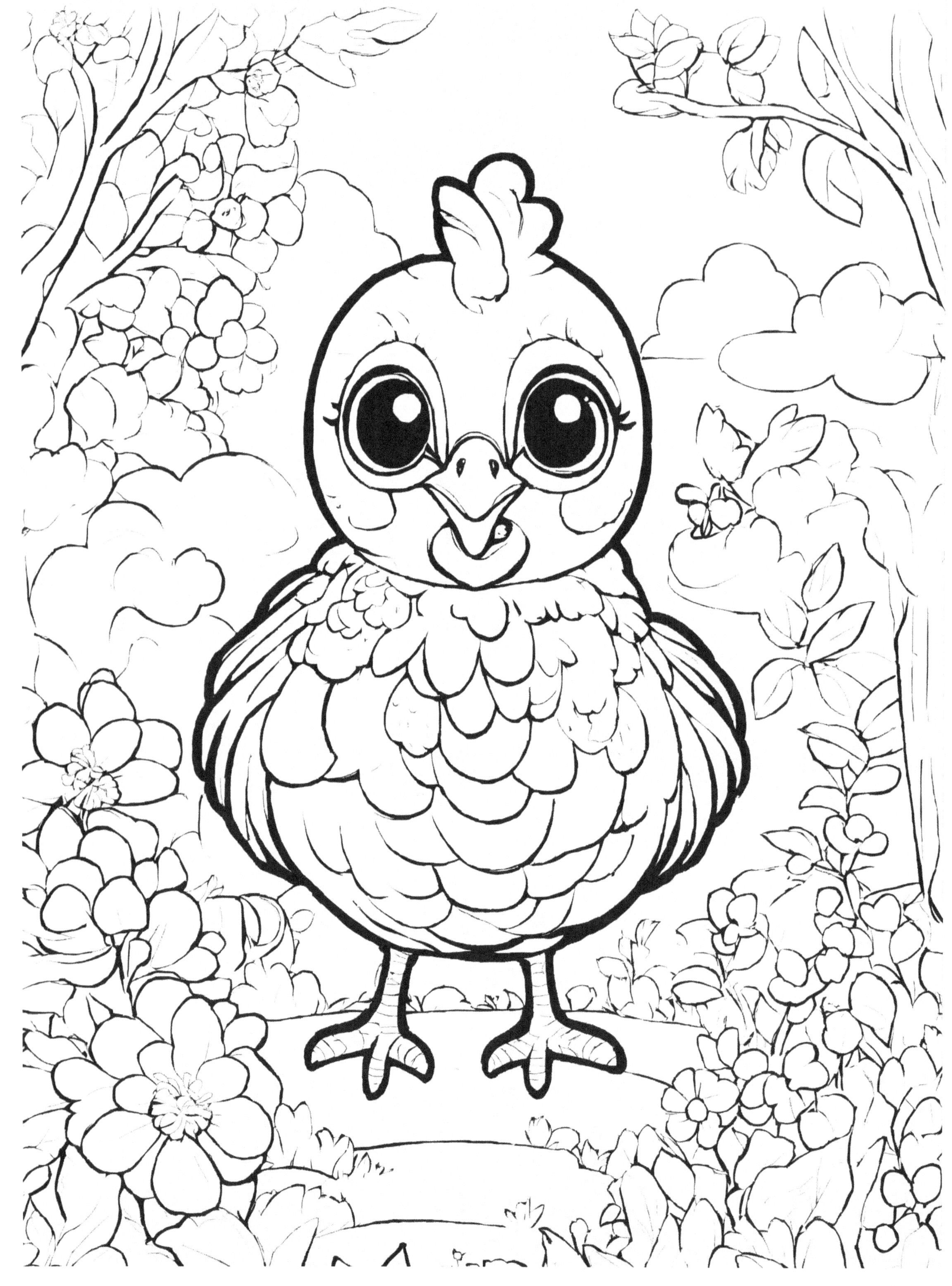

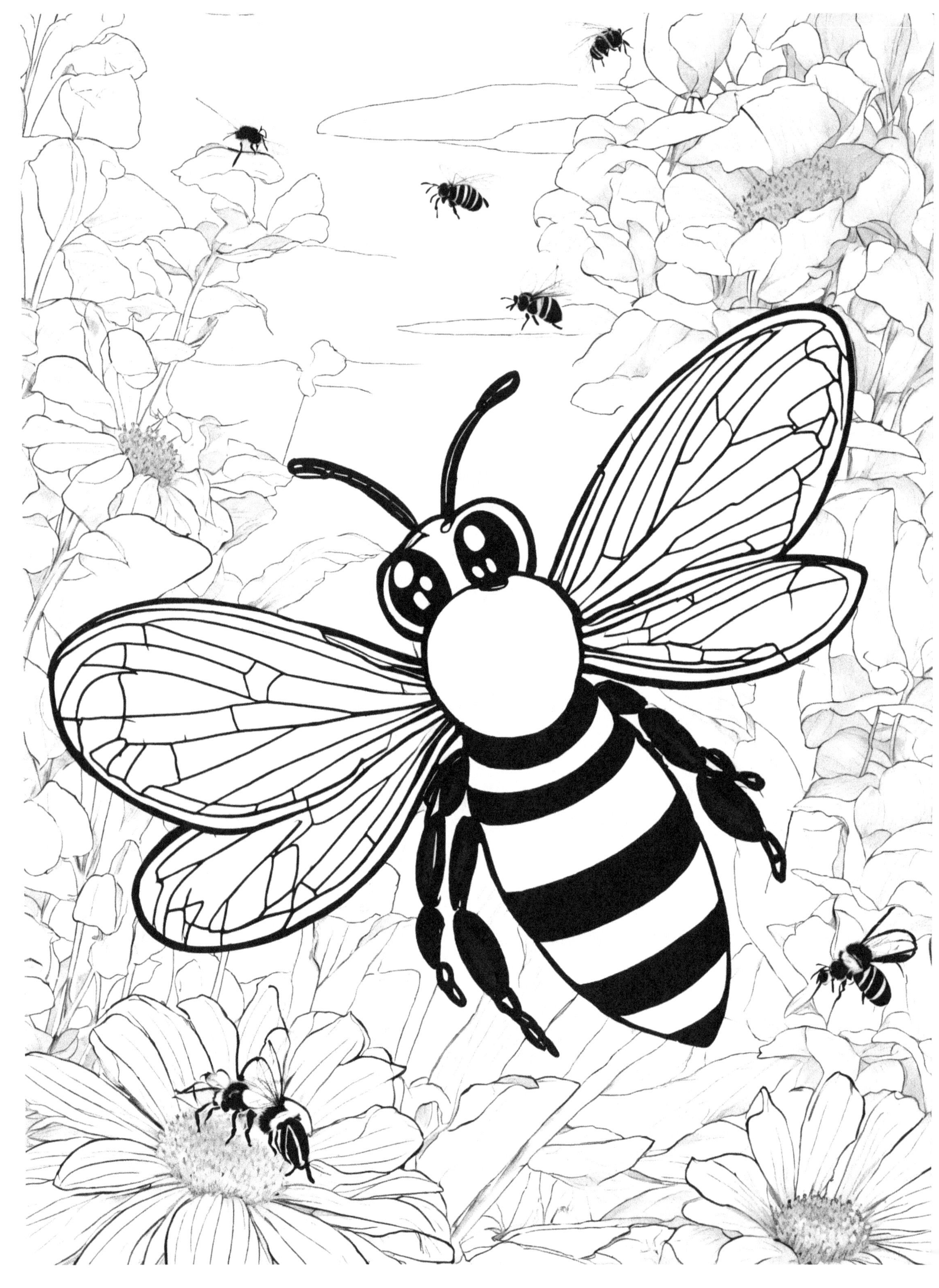

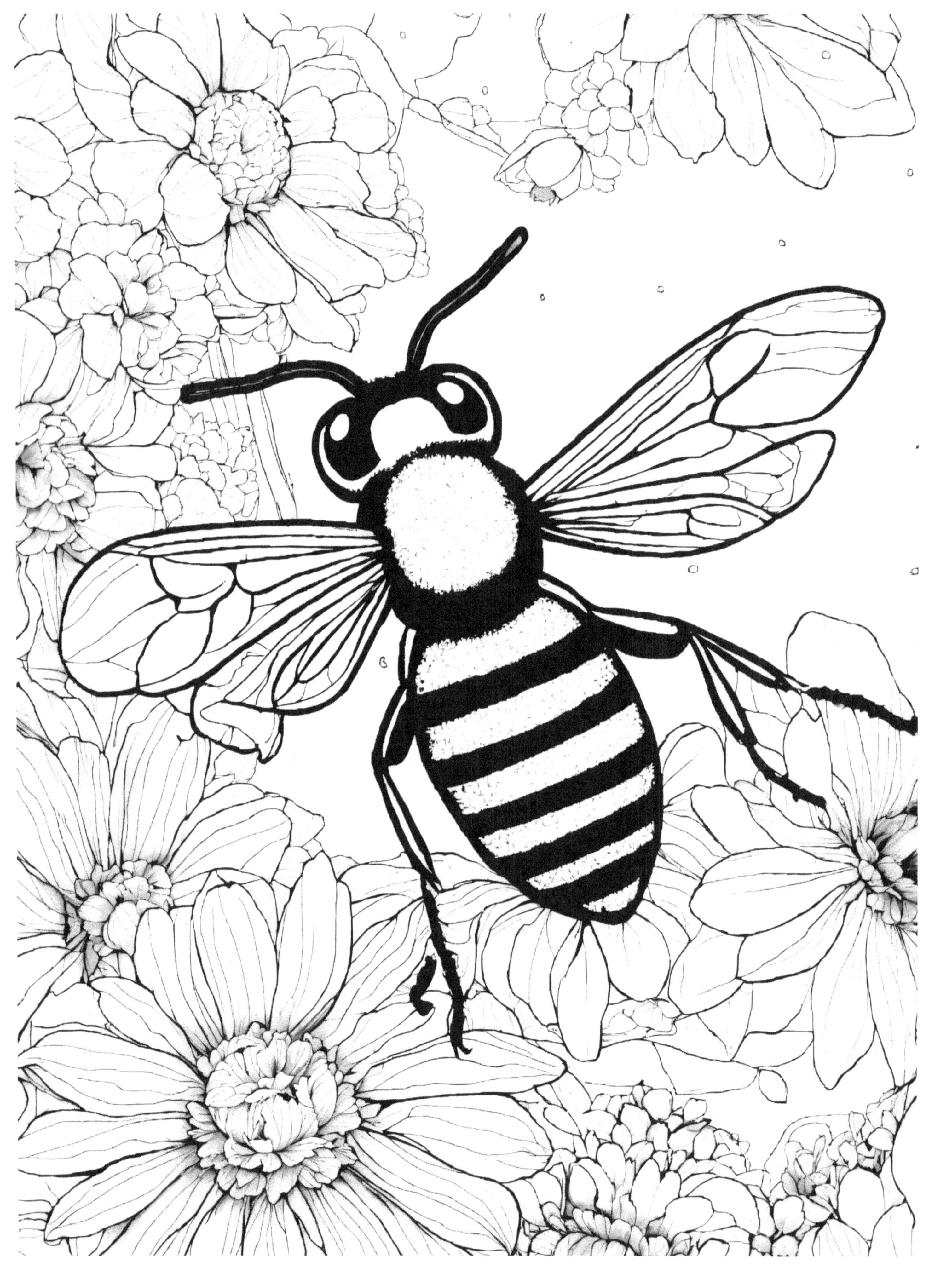

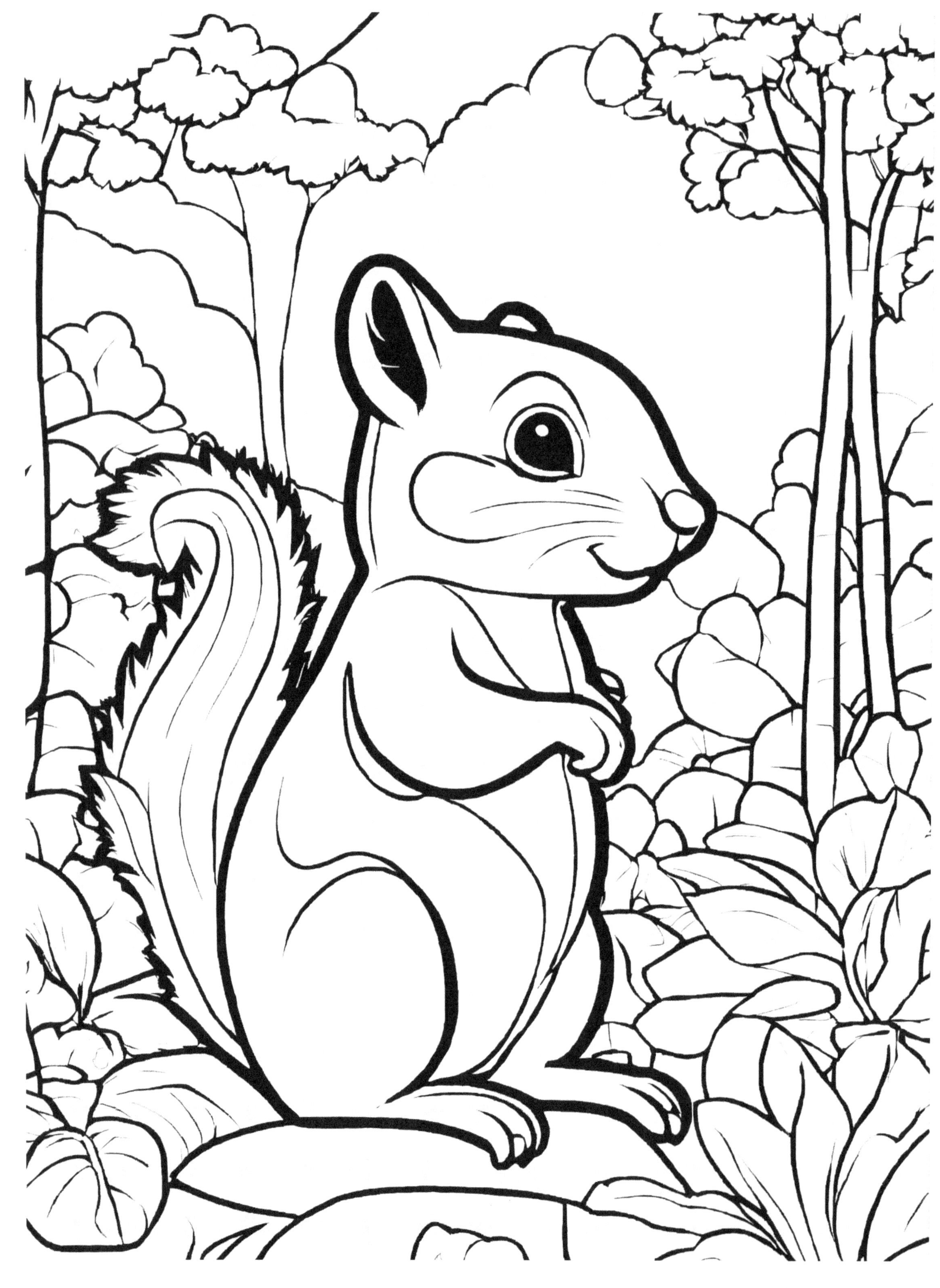

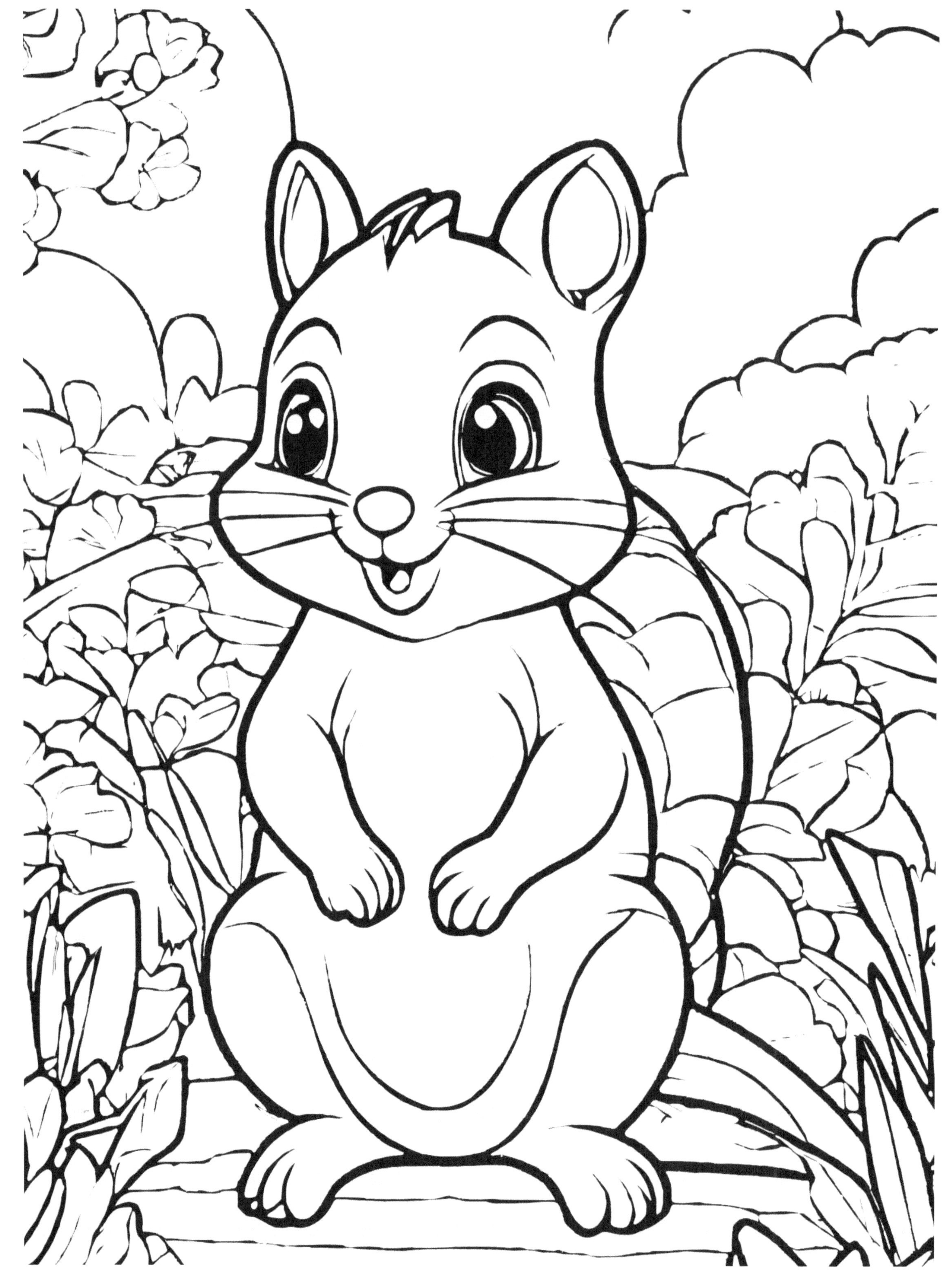

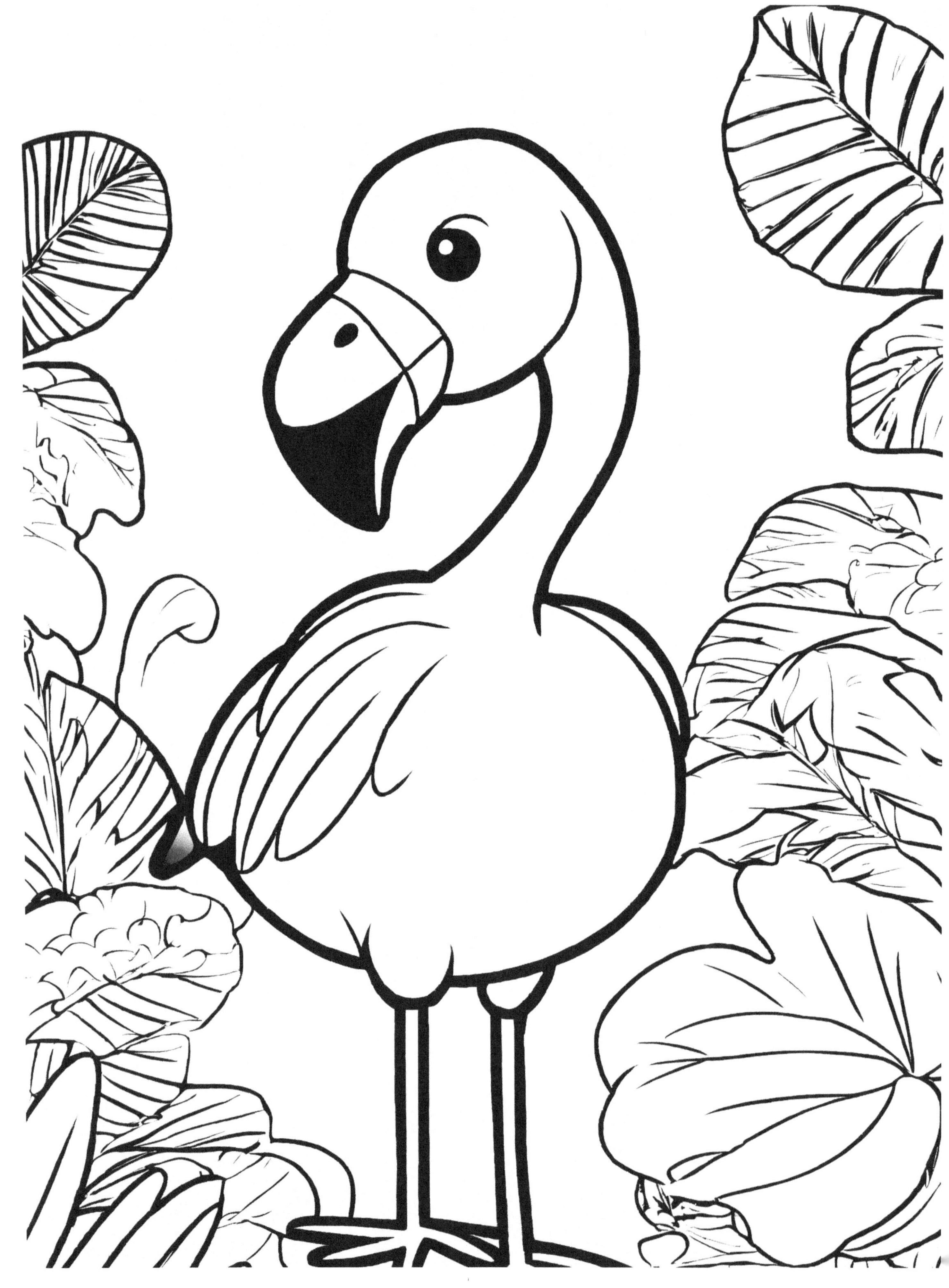

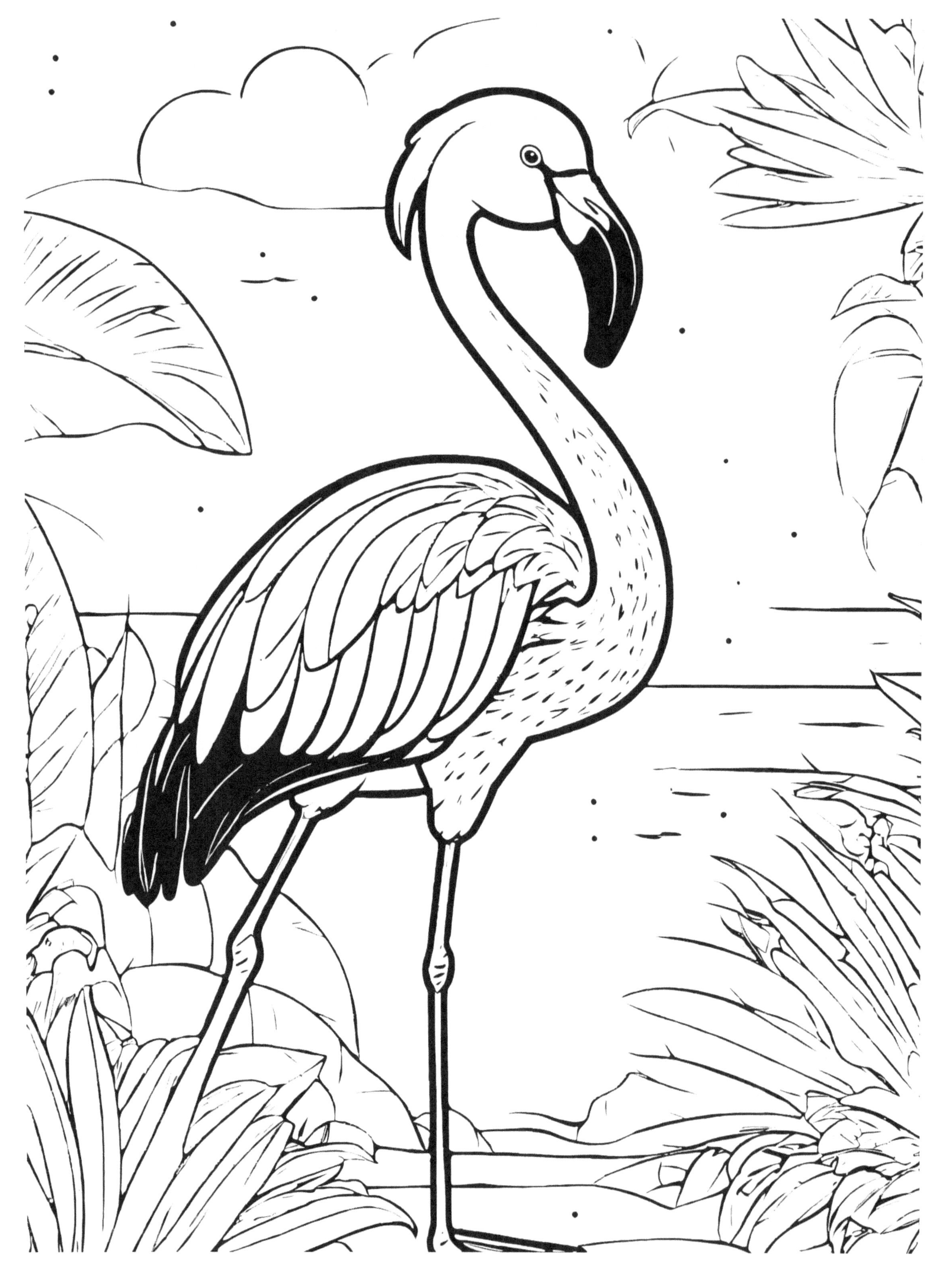

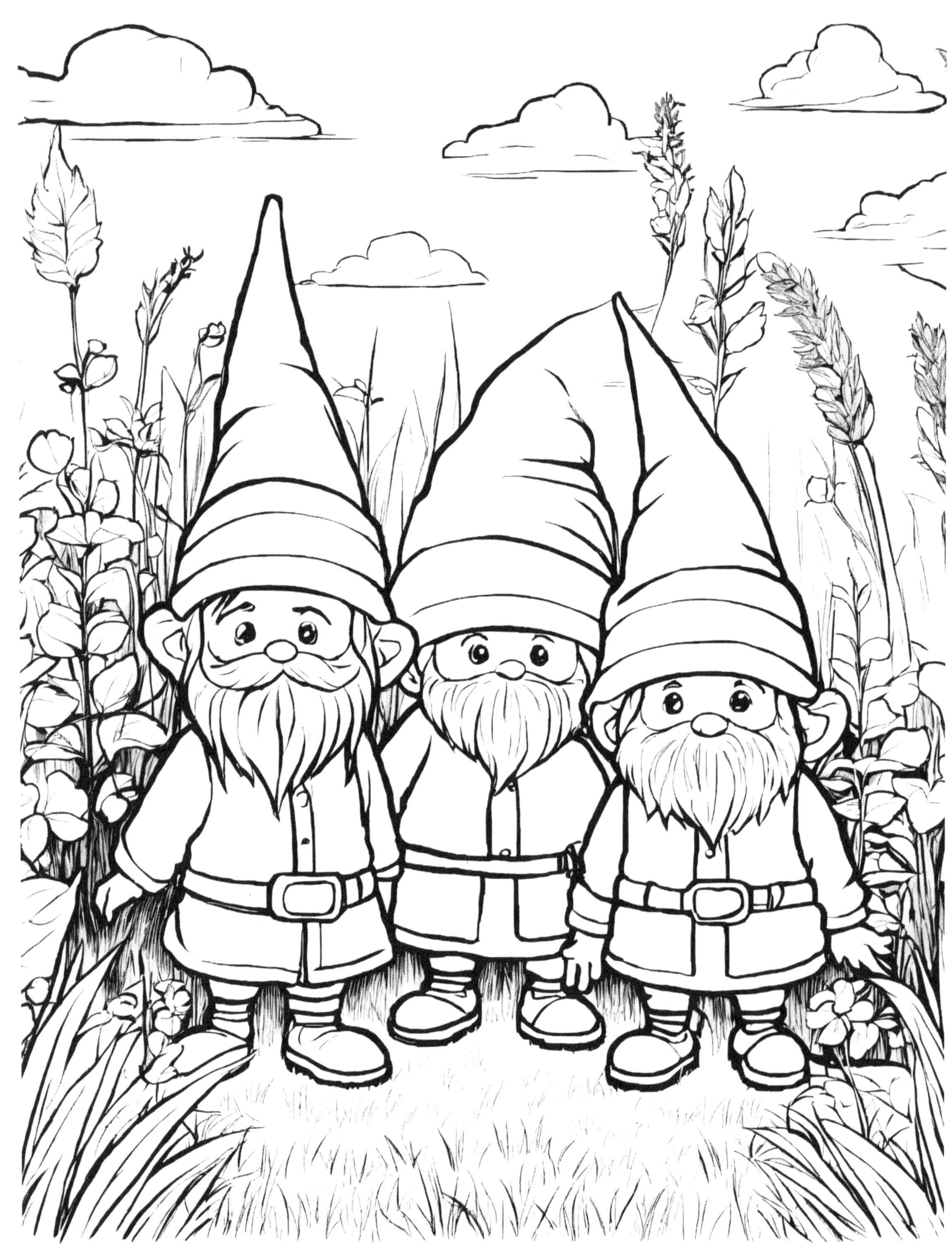

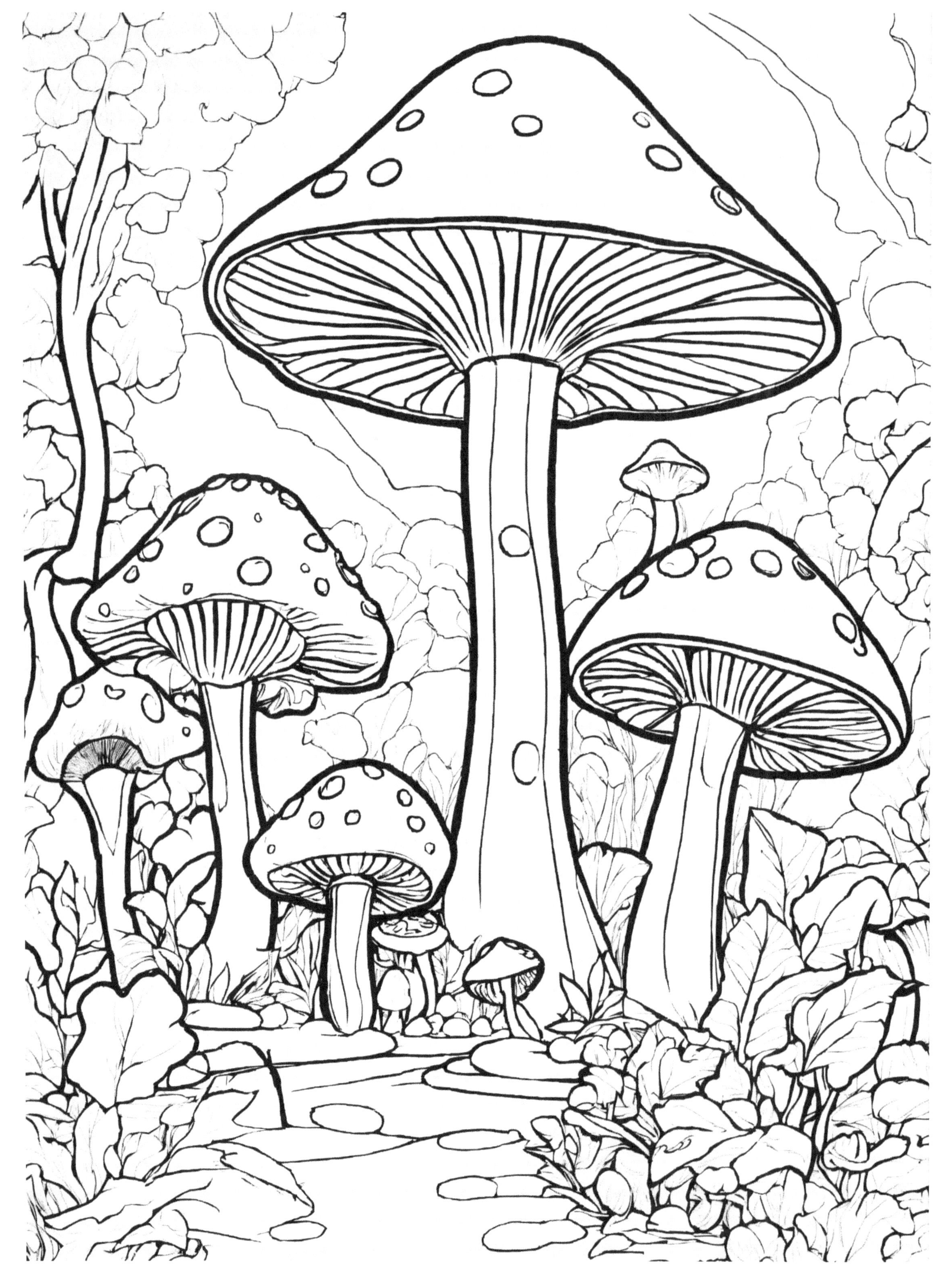

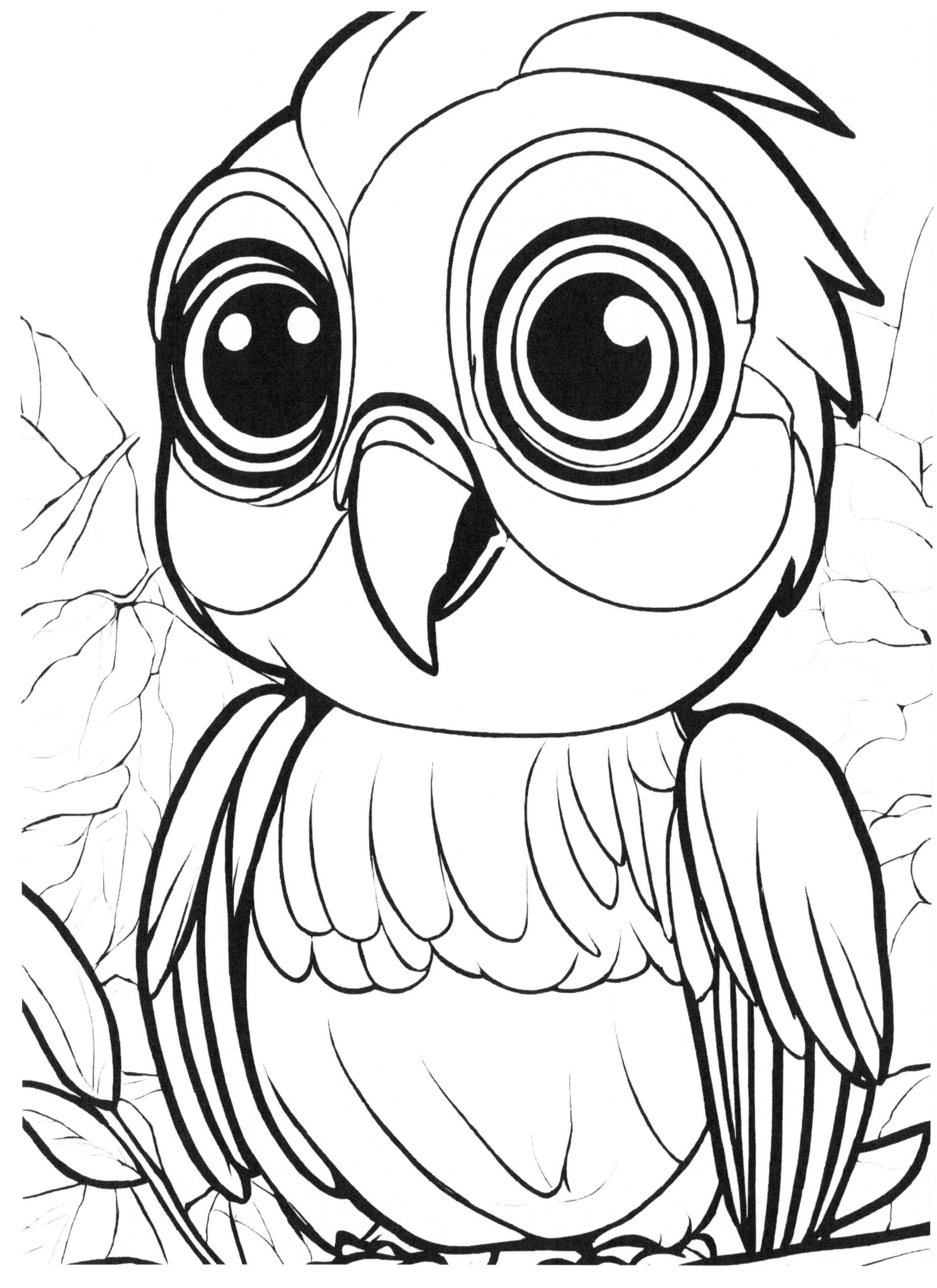

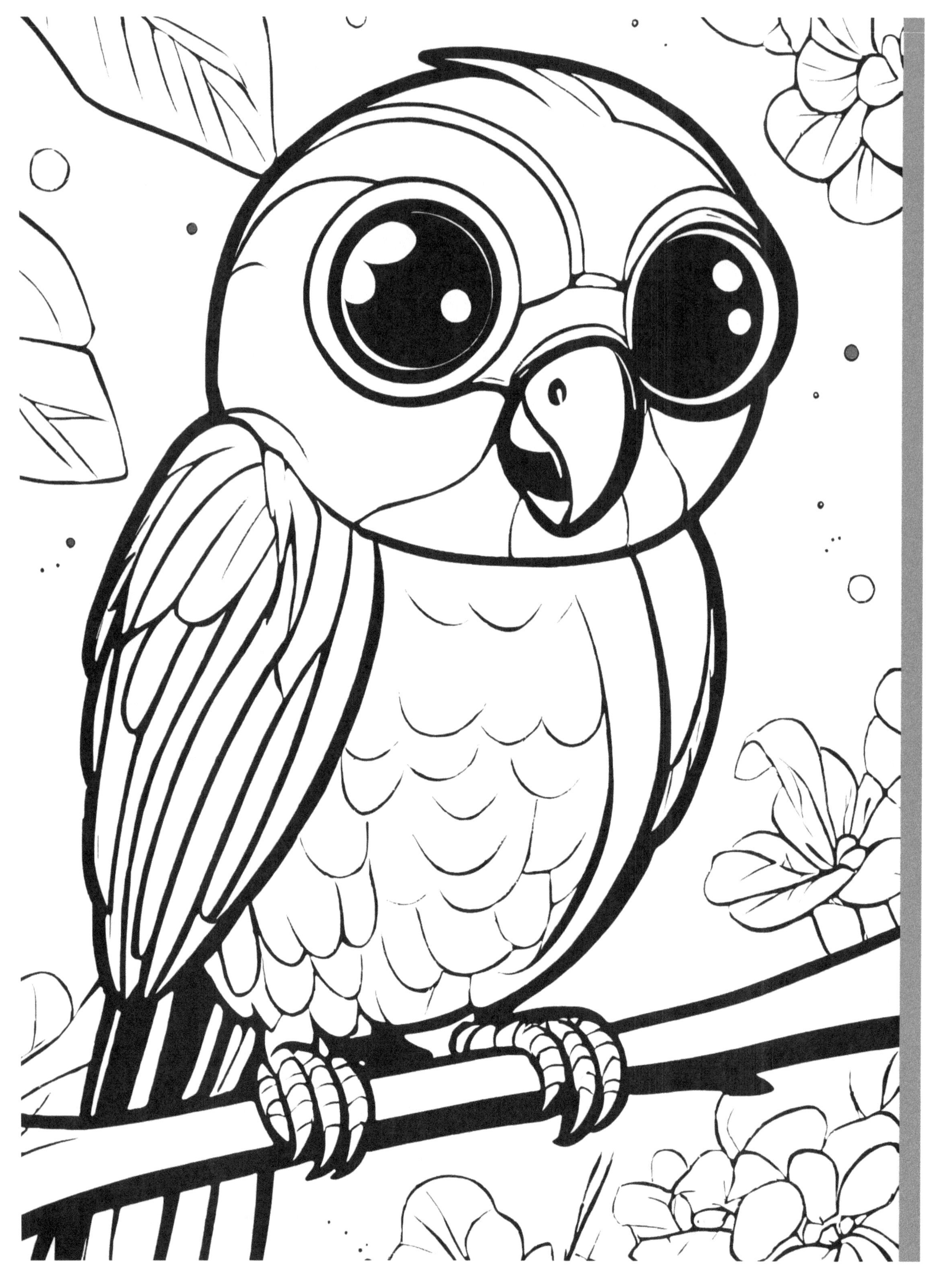

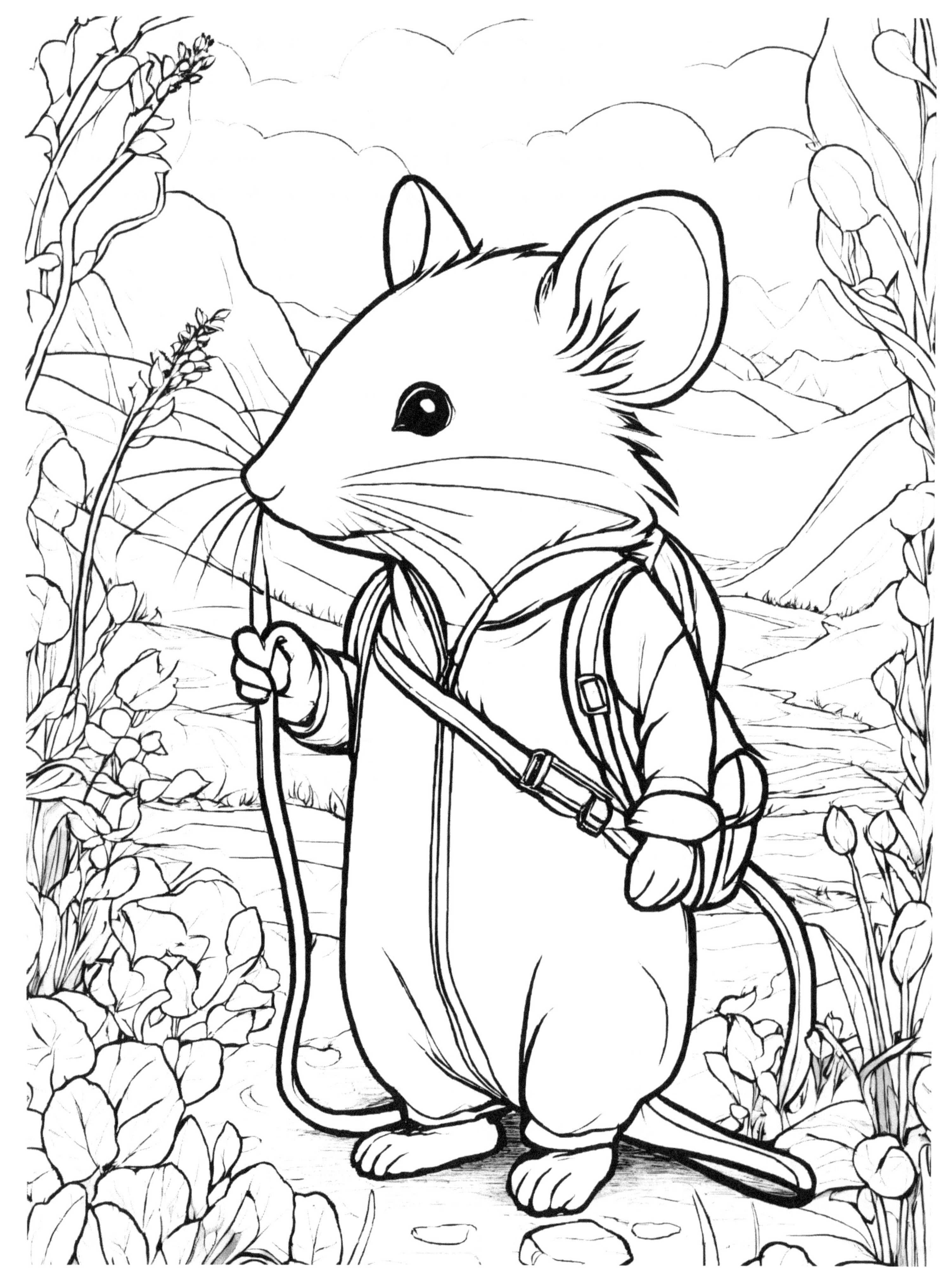